# The Left Behind Fantasy

# Other Books by William Powell Tuck

The Way For All Seasons

Facing Grief and Death

The Struggle for Meaning (editor)

Knowing God: Religious Knowledge in the Theology of John Baillie

Our Baptist Tradition

Ministry: An Ecumenical Challenge (editor)

Getting Past the Pain

A Glorious Vision

The Bible as Our Guide for Spiritual Growth (editor)

Authentic Evangelism

The Lord's Prayer Today

Through the Eyes of a Child

Christmas Is for the Young . . . Whatever Their Age

Love as a Way of Living

The Compelling Faces of Jesus

The Meaning of the Ten Commandments Today

# The Left Behind Fantasy

*The Theology Behind the* Left Behind *Tales*

WILLIAM POWELL TUCK

RESOURCE *Publications* • Eugene, Oregon

THE LEFT BEHIND FANTASY
The Theology Behind the *Left Behind* Tales

Copyright © 2010 William Powell Tuck. All rights reserved. Except for brief quotations in critical publications or reviews, no part of this book may be reproduced in any manner without prior written permission from the publisher. Write: Permissions, Wipf and Stock Publishers, 199 W. 8th Ave., Suite 3, Eugene, OR 97401.

Resource Publications
An Imprint of Wipf and Stock Publishers
199 W. 8th Ave., Suite 3
Eugene, OR 97401
www.wipfandstock.com

ISBN 13: 978-1-60899-277-5

Manufactured in the U.S.A.

Some scripture quotations are from the Revised Standard Version of the Bible (RSV), copyright 1946, 1952 © 1971, 1973, by the Division of Christian Education of the National Council of Churches of Christ in the USA.

Some scripture quotations are from the New Revised Standard Version of the Bible (NRSV), copyright ©1989 by the Division of Christian Education of the National Council of the Churches of Christ in the USA.

Some scripture quotations are from the King James Version of the Bible (KJV), in the public domain.

Some scripture quotations are from The New English Bible (NEB). Copyright © the Delegates of the Oxford University Press and the Syndics of the Cambridge University Press, 1961, 1970.

Echoes of Eternity: Listening to the Fathers ©2004 Community of Jesus. Used by permission of Paraclete Press. Available from Paraclte Press, www.paracletepress.com <http://www.paracletepress.com/> or 800-451-5006
Used by permission of Paraclete Press.

*To*
*Paul Simmons*
*Outstanding ethicist, professor, writer and preacher,*
*and good friend for forty years*

# Contents

*Foreword by John Killinger  ix*
*Preface  xiii*

1  An Overview  1

2  A Prelude to Doomsday  5

3  Left Behind Biblical Terminology  24

4  Alternative Understandings  49

5  Discerning the Truth  69

6  Critiquing the Theology Behind the *Left Behind* Novels  97

7  Moving Forward Faithfully  129

*Bibliography*  145
*Subject/Name Index*  153

# Foreword

In a day when many critics are calling into question the very survival of the book industry, we have had three of the greatest blockbuster novels or series of novels in all of publishing history--Dan Brown's *The Da Vinci Code*, J. K. Rowling's Harry Potter series, and Tim LaHaye and Jerry Jenkins' *Left Behind* stories--and, curiously, every one of them has been in one way or another concerned with Christianity.

The plot of Brown's *Da Vinci Code*, because it contained links to the library of early Christian gospels unearthed at Nag Hammadi in the 1950s, turned on the possibility that Jesus was married and had a child, and that his wife and child escaped to France after he was crucified and became the basis for a secret order of Christians whose existence was opposed by the papacy.

The seven Harry Potter books, as I have shown in *God, the Devil, and Harry Potter* and *The Life, Death, and Resurrection of Harry Potter*, owe their entire plot structure to the biblical story of Jesus and his struggle against the Prince of Darkness. While many Christians denounced Rowling's stories as unfit for children, their principal readers, because they were filled with witches and supernatural happenings, Rowling was actually retelling the Christian myth in her clever narratives about an orphan boy whose love for others eventually saved the entire world from the machinations of the evil Lord Voldemort.

LaHaye and Jenkins' *Left Behind* books are all loosely based on early Judeo-Christian writings about the end of the world, principally the weird and enigmatic passages from the book of Revelation, which Bruce Metzger, one of the most revered biblical scholars of recent times, warned in his book *Breaking the Code* should not be "isolated and interpreted with wooden literalism."[1] The real emphasis on the Last Days in Christian doctrine, he said, "is moral rather than chronological," with each genera-

---

1. Metzger, *Breaking the Code*, 11.

tion living with the imperative to behave accountably before God as if it were the final one.[2]

Which brings us to the subject of *this* book, *The Left Behind Fantasy*.

It is very clear in both Dan Brown's and J. K. Rowling's books that they are creating fiction and have merely utilized certain ingredients from Christian history and theology as provocative elements of their writings. What is not so clear in the LaHaye-Jenkins novels is this accepted demarcation between fiction and reality. They have in fact intentionally blurred the lines between the two, suggesting that, while their stories are obviously fictitious, they are more-or-less play-by-play descriptions of the end of the world as they have discerned them in the Scriptures.

G. K. Chesterton, the essayist, once observed that while St. John the Evangelist beheld many strange and wonderful creatures in his vision, "he saw no creature so wild as one of his own commentators."[3] Were Chesterton still alive in the day of the *Left Behind* series, he would no doubt place its authors, LaHaye and Jenkins, in the very front rank of wild commentators, for it would be hard to imagine a more flagrantly wrong-headed series than the one they have published.

They did not of course originate the brand of eschatology that flourishes in their books. Known as dispensational premillennialism, it already had a broad following from the notes of C. I. Scofield's long-popular study Bible, and then, in 1970, from the publication of Hal Lindsey's megabestseller *The Late Great Planet Earth*. LaHaye was copping Scofield and Lindsey's message long before he and Jenkins began producing the novels for which they are so well known. As is sometimes the curious way of things, few people now remember Hal Lindsey and almost everybody recognizes the names of LaHaye and Jenkins.

It could be argued that we deserve the apocalypticism-on-steroids of the *Left Behind* books if only because educated, upscale Christians have in recent years paid so little attention to the eschatological sayings of Jesus and the hurry-because-the-times-are-uncertain note in other biblical writings, especially the book of Revelation. For years we have stuck to safer grounds for our preaching and teaching, thus deserting the whole apocalyptic field to the storefront preachers and biblical interpreters who

---

2. Ibid., 105.
3. Chesterton, *Orthodoxy*, 17.

always exhibit more imagination than common sense. Few people paid any attention to LaHaye when he was a TV evangelist. When he hooked up with Jenkins, a journalist, he turned his end-time scenarios into pot-boiling novels about the final days of human civilization.

William Tuck is right to highlight the added impetus given to the *Left Behind* books by 9/11 and its aftermath. Our times are extraordinarily charged with the electricity of interfaith wars, heightened airport security, a parade of bombings in crowded international cities, and, more recently, a nearly catastrophic global economic meltdown. To many ordinary Christians, these must indeed seem like the Last Days, when cultures are in collision and the very fabric of human civilization is coming unraveled, if not being forcefully ripped asunder.

Thank God for a voice like Bill Tuck's willing to take on such a popular series and point out with quiet patience and intellectual acumen where it goes off the track and how dangerous its assumptions become when it does. I have known Bill for a long time and have always regarded him as one of the most serious and learned pastors of our time. Following the pattern of scholarly preachers set by such giants as A. J. Gossip, George Buttrick, and Harry Emerson Fosdick, he has always read omnivorously and prepared his sermons with fastidious attention to the biblical texts on one hand and modern culture on the other.

It is easy to imagine the growing indignation he must have felt for the arrogant, haphazard manner in which LaHaye and Jenkins presented their fictional account of the end of civilization, and for the way vast numbers of Christians have accepted that account as a literal blueprint of what is actually going to happen. He probably faced parishioners in his own congregations who believed that the *Left Behind* stories were exact, unimpeachable records of what will transpire in the final days.

It is never easy to play Cassandra to any popular movement, and Bill won't earn any thanks from millions of LaHaye and Jenkins devotees, many of whom will undoubtedly accuse him of jealousy, irreverence, and a shameful lack of spirituality. Some may even paint him as a tool of Satan commissioned to write a book that would cause weaker and less committed Christians to lose their way along life's rugged path. And given the nature of things, his book will probably not sell even a hundred copies for every ten thousand *Left Behind* books now in print.

But knowing Bill as I do, that will not matter to him. What does and always has mattered to him is fidelity to the gospel and a certain mental doggedness in the attempt to discuss and understand its real meaning for our age. And eventually, when time has revealed which things from our age were true and faithful and which were false or merely preposterous, I have no doubt that he will be gloriously vindicated for his attempt to set the record straight and for liberating at least a few readers from the interpretations of LaHaye and Jenkins.

So I congratulate him now, on the eve of *The Left Behind Fantasy*'s publication, and wish, as the poet Leigh Hunt did for Abou Ben Adhem, that his tribe might greatly increase!


John Killinger
author of *The Life, Death, and Resurrection of Harry Potter*
and *If Christians Were Really Christian*

# Preface

SINCE I WAS BOY, I have always loved to read fiction. Every Christmas when I was a child I received a book or two under the tree like Mary Mapes Dodge's *Hans Brinker,* Robert Louis Stevenson's *Kidnapped,* Zane Grey's *The Last of the Plainsmen,* Louisa May Alcott's *Little Men*, Charles Nordhoff and James Hall's *Mutiny on the Bounty,* Samuel L. Clemens, *Tom Sawyer*, Howard Pyle's *The Merry Adventures of Robin Hood* and many others. Later I began to read the works of Albert Camus, Ernest Hemingway, William Faulkner, Franz Kafka, Boris Pasternak, Alan Paton, John Steinbeck, Mark Twain, John Updike, H.G. Wells and more recently the popular writings of John Grisham, James Michener, Pat Conroy, Mitch Albom, Dean Koontz and many others.

When I was in high school and considering going into the ministry, I read my first "Christian" novel, James Street's *The High Calling*, the story about a minister of a large city church who accepts the call from a much smaller milltown church. I have read much better "Christian" fiction since my first encounter with that kind of literature. I have explored such Christian fiction as Lew Wallace's *Ben Hur*, the fantasies and science fiction of C.S. Lewis' *Till We Have Faces, The Pilgrim's Regress, Out of the Silent Planet. Perelandra,* and *That Hideous Strength,* as well as J.R.R. Tolkien's *The Lord of the Rings,* Georges Bernanos' *The Dairy of a Country Priest,* Graham Greene's *The Power and the Glory,* Joseph F. Girzone's *Joshua,* Will Campbell's *Brother to a Dragonfly,* Frederick Buechner's *Son of Laughter* and others of his novels, John Killinger's *Jessie: A Novel,* Dan Brown's *The Da Vinci Code* and others. Good Christian fiction has always had a special appeal for me.

When I first heard about the *Left Behind* fiction, I got mixed reports from readers. Some thought they were good, imaginative adventure stories based on teachings from the Book of Revelation; others saw them as a type of science fiction. While still others detested them or chose not to read them, I decided to see for myself. As I began to read them, I knew that they had created a wide reading audience and had drawn reviews from credited, national magazines and newspapers. I discovered that they had an interesting adventure plot, beginning especially with *The Tribulation Force*, which reminded me of an old Mission Impossible theme. The more I read them, and I did read all sixteen of the novels, including the three prequels, *The Rising, The Regim* and *The Rapture*, (which I found the least interesting of them all), and the final volume, *Kingdom Come: The Final Victory*, or I listened to them as recorded books, I began to look carefully at the biblical and theological premises on which they were based. I read several of them more than once and read other writings by Tim LaHaye to see what his theological frame of reference was. This book is a result of my study. I invite you to explore the theology behind the *Left Behind* novels with me.

I want to express my appreciation to Richard B. Vinson, former Professor of New Testament and Dean at the Baptist Theological Seminary at Richmond, Virginia, for reading the manuscript and offering several suggestions. A special word of appreciation is expressed to my daughter, Catherine Whitty, who typed this manuscript from my "Hieroglyphics" while taking care of her three small children. It was a special act of daughterly love. I also want to thank Sandra Bundick for her help in getting my manuscript in the final form for publication.

1

# An Overview

I WANT TO INVITE you to go with me on a journey as we travel together to see if we can grasp the biblical and theological foundation that forms the basis for the *Left Behind* novels. Tim LaHaye has been selected in the 2005 *Time Magazine's* listing of "The 25 Most Influential Evangelicals in America."[1] The *Left Behind* novels, written by LaHaye and Jerry Jenkins, *Time* notes, have "set the image that many people—believers and non-believers alike—now have about how the world will end."[2] Former president, Jimmy Carter, states that the fundamentalist "rapture" views of the "end times" and interpretations like those of the *Left Behind* series have influenced the views of many toward Israel, the Holy Land, Islam, the Iraqi war in their agenda to try to determine what is happening in that part of the world to "hasten" the rapture. "It is the injection of these beliefs into America's governmental policies that is a cause for concern,"[3] Carter states. In a similar vein, Kevin Phillips argues that the unprecedented political role of George W. Bush's administration has shaped domestic and foreign policy in apocalyptic and religious perspectives. "The implication of domestic and international agenda," he believes, "seems to be driven by religious motivation and biblical world views."[4] He details this at great length in Part II of his book on page ninety-nine and following. Many of these religious/political views have been drawn from interpretations like those depicted in the *Left Behind* theology. LaHaye and Jenkins's view about the end of the world is heralded by some as the basic understand-

---

1. "The 25 Most Influential Evangelicals in America," 39.
2. Ibid.
3. Carter, *Our Endangered Values*, 114.
4. Phillips, *American Theocracy*, ix. See especially Part II, 99 ff.

ing of what the Bible teaches about the end.[5] "In terms of its impact on Christianity," (referring to the *Left Behind* novels and their kids books, CDs and other items) Jerry Falwell declared that "it's probably greater than that of any other book in modern times, outside the Bible."[6] That is a bold assertion and underscores the reason we need to examine carefully the teachings on which these novels are based.

## QUESTIONS TO PONDER

Questions such as the following need to be raised and answered, if possible. What has provoked this special interest in the end times? Are the concepts in the novels based on solid biblical and theological interpretations that are affirmed by most biblical scholars or are their views supported by only a few? Are there other views that can help to explain the Book of Revelation and the other teachings about what the end of the world will be like? As we seek to understand books like Revelation, Ezekiel and their teachings, are we open to the best and finest biblical scholars have to teach us? Should our faith be based on fear and dread of the future or founded on the love and assurance of the God we have seen revealed in Jesus Christ? Other questions will likely occur to you as we travel through these chapters, but these offer us some pointers as we begin.

## A SKETCH OF THE MAIN CHARACTERS

Some readers may not have read the *Left Behind* novels and might find it helpful to have a brief sketch of some of the main characters in the stories. The leading hero, Rayford Steele, who is in his mid-forties, is presented in the first novel in the series, *Left Behind,* as the 747 captain for Pan-Continental Air Lines. His wife, Irene and son, Raymie, were taken in the Rapture to Heaven and he and his daughter, Chloe, were "left behind." Later, after Rayford becomes a believer, he is an original member of the Tribulation Force, which is a group of believers seeking to reach others for Christ and contend with the Antichrist and his evil forces. His daughter, Chloe, is in her early twenties and a former student at Stanford University. She is one of the original members of the Tribulation Force after she becomes a believer. She eventually marries Buck Williams and they are the parents of a son, Kenny Bruce. She acts as the CEO of the

---

5. "The 25 Most Influential Evangelicals in America," 39.
6. Ibid.

International Commodity Co-op which is the underground network for the Christians located in a "safe house."

Cameron Williams, nick-named "Buck", probably in his early thirties, is introduced in the first novel as the senior writer for *Global Weekly*, an international news magazine. After his conversion, he becomes an original member of the Tribulation Force and the editor of *Truth,* a cyber magazine. Buck marries Chloe soon after they both become believers. Hattie Durham was originally a flight attendant on Pan-Continental 747 and the person with whom Rayford Steele considered having an affair. She later became a personal assistant and was engaged to Nicolae Carpathia. When she became pregnant with his child, he poisoned her and she had a miscarriage. Bruce Barnes, Visitation Pastor at New Hope Village Church in Mount Prospect, Illinois, is the only staff member in the church who was not taken in the Rapture. This was the church where Rayford's family was a member and Rayford attended occasionally. Bruce later acknowledged that he was not really a believer but only pretended to be a Christian. Following the Rapture, Bruce becomes a believer by listening to the tape the former senior pastor, Dr. Vernon Billings, left, and then he becomes the chief preacher and pastor at the church to help guide others to believe in the Rapture and become a believer. He is the person who shares his testimony and the tape about the Rapture with Rayford and Chloe. Chang Wong is the Christian "mole" at Global Community Headquarters in New Babylon (the Antichrist Center) and in love with Naomi Tiberias, a computer whiz.

Nicolae Jetty Carpathia, the Antichrist, was at the beginning of the novels the president of Romania, who became the Secretary-General of the United Nations and eventually the self appointed potentate of the Global Community in New Babylon. He was assassinated by Chaim Rosenzweig but three days later was resurrected before a world wide TV audience at his Global Palace. Leon Fortunato, the False Prophet, was the Supreme Commander of the Global Community Forces and the major supporter and instrument for Carpathia's bidding. He later became the new "religious" leader, the Father of Carpathianism that heralded Carpathia as the risen god who had to be worshipped by all or they would be put to death. Peter Matthews was seen first as a Roman Catholic cardinal from the Cincinnati archdiocese. He was later appointed as Pontifex Maximus or Peter II, the head of Enigma Babylon One World Faith.

Two noted Jewish leaders in the series are Tsion Ben-Judah and Dr. Chaim Rosenzweig. Ben-Judah was a rabbinical scholar and Israeli statesman who was converted to Christ after a careful study of the Scriptures and surprisingly acknowledged his conversion on an international television program to the consternation of other Jewish leaders. Buck helped him escape from Israel to the United States where he became the spiritual leader and teacher of the Tribulation Force and broadcasted his Christian teachings daily to a billion viewers. Chaim Rosenzweig was an Israeli botanist and statesman who discovered a scientific formula that enabled the deserts in Israel to bloom. He was awarded a Nobel Prize for his scientific work. He was the person who assassinated Carpathia.

In a sort of preamble briefing at the front of the novels, beginning with *Assassins,* the sixth in the series, the authors provide a succinct description of the various persons in the stories. This sketch provides a helpful resource in understanding the major characters in the novels. A recent book entitled The *Authorized Left Behind Handbook* by Tim LaHaye, Jerry Jenkins and Sandi L. Swanson, published in March of 2005 by Tyndale Publishing, provides a behind the scenes look at the characters, a brief digest of the books, facts and information from the books, and interviews with the authors. This might be a helpful introductory resource for the reader.

As we examine the *Left Behind* novels and the non-fictional writings of LaHaye and others for their biblical and theological beliefs, I hope this brief overview of the characters will offer a helpful perspective to orientate the reader for what lies ahead in your spiritual expedition through these pages. Let's travel together in pursuit of understanding the biblical teachings about the "end times" and living out its teachings in our lives.

## 2

## A Prelude to Doomsday

A RECENT CASUAL WALK into a Christian bookstore in my section of town revealed the following books focusing on the end time emphasis: *Ancient Prophecy and Modern Day Conspiracy Collide* by Michael D. Evans, *The Last Day* by James Landis, *God's Promises of Prophecy* by Jack Van Impe, *Beginning of the End* by John Hagee, *Seven Signs of the End Times* by Mark Hitchcock, *Final Dawn Over Jerusalem* by John Hagee, *End-Time Visions: The Doomsday Obsession* by Richard Abanes, *The Rise of Babylon* by Charles H. Dyer, *Prosperity and the Coming Apocalypse* by Jim Baker, *The Final Quest and the Torch and the Sword* by Rick Joyner, *Escape the Coming Night* by David Jeremiah, *Storm Clouds on the Horizon: Bible Prophecy and the Current Middle East Crisis*, edited by Charles H. Dyer, *The End of the Age* by Pat Robertson, *Are We Living in the End of Time?*, *The Rapture: Who will Face the Tribulation?*, *Revelation Unveiled and Prophecy Study Bible* all by Tim LaHaye, *The Truth Behind Left Behind* by Mark Hitchcock and Thomas Ice and the *Left Behind* novels by Tim LaHaye and Jerry B. Jenkins and other end times fiction.

All of these books brought to my mind the familiar cartoon and occasional television image of the bearded man in a long white robe who was seen carrying a sign that read, "The End Is Near!" as he walked up and down a busy sidewalk somewhere in downtown USA. All of these books reflecting on various dimensions of the end times made me wonder if the old prophet wasn't correct.

Many volumes on the end times by various persons of different theological perspectives, but especially fundamentalists, have flooded the marketplace. There has always been an interest in the last day, prophecy and the *Book of Revelation*, but the publication of the *Left Behind* novels has awakened an interest in this area which defies the imagination. These novels seem to have created more interest than the prophecies of

Nostradamus and the writing of other "seers" into the future like Edgar Cayce and Jeane Dixon, with a biblical twist. The writers claim that the fictional series is based on sound biblical knowledge, and although the novels are fiction, the theology behind them is fact. I decided to read them to see if that in fact was factual.

When I mentioned to my friends, especially clergy friends, that I was reading the *Left Behind* series of novels, I always got a diffident smile and a clear retort, "I have never read any of *those* books and don't intend to!" But somebody certainly is! At this writing, over sixty-two million copies of the sixteen volumes have been sold. The initial book, *Left Behind*, has passed the eight million mark and many of the other volumes have sold over four million copies each and have been translated into thirty-four or more languages. The final volume, *Kingdom Come: The Final Victory*, also made the New York Times Best-Seller List in April, 2007. The official *Left Behind* series website is *www.leftbehind.com* and offers links to a prophecy club, a twice-monthly newsletter, devotional guides, a resource center, recommended resources (articles, books, videos, etc.) about the "last days", discipleship guidance, scriptural bases for their beliefs, various articles interpreting the Book of Revelation giving the location of Babylon and noting the meaning of words like rapture, Armageddon, the Antichrist, where and how to purchase copies of the various *Left Behind* books and much more. *A Visual Guide to the Left Behind Series* and *Left Behind Discussion Guides* offer guidance to help readers navigate their way through the events of the end times in the books and the series.

Five of the first eleven books in the *Left Behind* series have made No. 1 on the *New York Times* bestseller list as well as *USA Today*, *The Wall Street Journal* and *Publishers Weekly*. When the final volume, *Glorious Appearing*, was published in 2004, in less than a month it was No. 1 on the *USA Today* bestseller list and soon was on other national listings. The first prequel, *The Rising*, was published in March, 2005 and the second, *The Regime*, published in December, 2005, and *The Rapture*, the final prequel, published in June of 2006, were written to tell the story of what some of the "characters" were doing before the Rapture. The final novel in the series, *Kingdom Come*, dealing with the Millennium, was published in April of 2007. *Left Behind: The Sequel* has also been projected. LaHaye and Jenkins have already published several volumes in a new series called "The Jesus Chronicles" which is written from the perspective of one of the disciples like Mark, John or Luke. LaHaye has already linked with another writer of thrillers, Grey Dinallo, and produced the first novel, *Babylon Rising*, in a new series. The second in the series is *The Secret of Ararat*, written with or by Bob Phillips. This new fiction series is to be fast-paced action thrillers based on biblical prophecies, which were not covered in the *Left Behind* novels, LaHaye noted. This first volume was published in October of 2003 by Bantom Books, a secular publisher. Jerry Jenkins has also started a new series called the "Underground Zealot Trilogy" with two novels already published, *Soon: The Beginning of the End* and *Silence: The Wrath of God Descends*.

Already a forty volume series based on the *Left Behind* novels has been published for children as well as comic books, two movies, a PC strategy game called Left Behind Eternal Forces, CDs, radio drama, calendars, audio and videotapes, including books on tapes and many other off-springs have appeared on the scene. National magazines like *Time* (July 1, 2002), *Newsweek* and others have had major articles on the *Left Behind* books. Television programs like 60 Minutes (February 8, 2004), 60 Minutes II (April 14, 2004), The Dennis Miller Show (July 1, 2004) and other national network and cable news shows have aired segments with Tim LaHaye and Jerry Jenkins, the writers of the series. The publication of the books and all of the "by products" have produced very lucrative sales of hundreds of millions of dollars for the authors and Tyndale House Publishers. The *Left Behind* books can be purchased not only in Christian bookstores but also at discount prices at places like Wal-Mart, Target and in many grocery and drug stores.

When I went to my local library to get a copy of the audio version of the book on tape, *Armageddon*, I discovered that eight people were ahead of me on the "hold list", and I had to wait months to get it. Later when I tried to renew the recorded book, I could not because of the large number who was waiting to get the book. According to research from the publishers of the series of books, Tyndale House, 84 percent of its readers are born again Christians, 16 percent are non-Christian and 4 percent called themselves atheists. The series is most popular with women (57 percent) who are married, between the ages of 25 and 54, college educated, born again evangelical Christians who live in the South, attend church weekly and pray and read the Bible more then the average person.[1]

The *Left Behind* fiction series is not the first or only novels to focus on the Christian view of the Rapture. In 1937 Forrest Loman Oilar

---

1. Holmes, "Final Book", 4.

wrote a novel entitled *Be Thou Prepared, for Jesus is Coming. Raptured, A Novel* by Ernest Angley was published in 1950 and in 1970 Salem Kirban published a novel entitled *666*, which went through fourteen printings. All of these novels bear similar themes to those in the *Left Behind* series and may have furnished "yeast" for the famous present day writers. The *Left Behind* movie was also not the first of the end time movies. In 1972 *A Thief in the Night* appeared which told about a woman who ignored the prophecies of the coming Rapture and her struggles to see whether she could still find her way to the truth and be spared. All of these novels and films depict a God who favors a selected few and shows disregard for what happens to innocent persons who are hurt or killed when the "saved ones" are snatched out of the world to be in Heaven with Christ.

Why has there been such an interest in this series of books and others that have focused on the "end times"? Why have books like *Left Behind* sold on the bestseller lists alongside works like Stephen King, Danielle Steel, or John Grisham? A recent poll by *Time/CNN* found that more than one-third of Americans stated that they were now paying more attention to how the news might relate to the end of the world and what the Bible revealed about the subject. The poll also revealed that 59 percent believed that the events predicted in Revelation were going to happen. Almost one-quarter thought that the September 11 attack was foretold by the Bible.[2]

## THE TERRORIST THREAT

Unfortunately people often wax hot and cold toward religion. When their health is good, life seems productive and they live without a great deal of misfortune and the world situation is stable and natural disasters are at a medium, then religion seems low on the scale of interest for many. On the other hand, when illness strikes, an accident occurs, fortunes fail or natural disasters or wars arise, or terrorism prevails, then many persons turn to religion or return to church. After the 9/11 attacks in 2001 when terrorists crashed planes into the twin towers of the New York's World Trade Center, the crash of an airplane into the Pentagon and a fourth plane crashed outside Pittsburg, church attendance on the following Sunday was high. In a few weeks, however, attendance dropped back to normal.

---

2. *Time* (July 1, 2002), 42.

*Desecration,* book nine in the *Left Behind* series, was published in October right after 9/11, and was the best selling novel of 2001. Sales of the books in the *Left Behind* series went up fifty percent after the attack. Interest was sharpened once again in the minds of many in their desire to know if the Bible predicted such terrorists' events and how we might prevent or avoid them. Terrorism remains a frightening and costly threat to many personally but also to the stability of the world, as many know it. The uncertainty of when and where another terrorist attack might happen and the possible use of chemical, biological or nuclear weapons or the contamination of our food and water resources contribute to the end time fears. The Iraq war, rather than easing the world's fears of international terrorism, has raised them to an alarming level.

The horrendous event of 9/11 was the most prominent of many terrorists' attacks over the last decades that have led many to believe that the world is approaching the "last days" and that the return of Christ is imminent. Some preachers and writers have seen the 9/11 attacks as one of many "signs" that the "end" was near. These doomsday prophets list other "signs" as the collapse of the Soviet Union, the sexual revolution with the dissolution of the traditional family and the rise of "gay marriages", other militant terrorists' attacks in Spain, Hong Kong, Israel, Iraq, Tokyo, Turkey, Russia and in other countries, the worldwide threat of AIDS, the global problems of pollution, the founding of the State of Israel, the secularism of society, especially in the United States and its "drift" away from the religious tradition of its "Founding Fathers", the rise of violent crime and the use of drugs, the Jamestown tragedy in November 1978, the deadly encounter between the FBI and religious radicals at Ruby Ridge, Idaho in 1993, the fiery holocaust of David Koresh's Branch Davidian Compound called Mt. Carmel at Waco, Texas in 1993, the bombing of the Alfred P. Murrah Federal Building in Oklahoma City with the death of 169 people in April 19, 1995, the genocide of thousands in Cambodia, Rwanda, Iraq and Sudan, the rapid rise of spiritualism and New Age religion, the Millennium in 2000, the overthrow of Saddam Hussein's reign in Iraq and his ultimate capture, the "sightings" of UFO's and many other signs.

Prophecy writers and preachers like Hal Lindsey, Pat Robertson, Jerry Falwell, John Hagee and Jack Van Impe have seen these events and others as "signs" which they have used to make their predictions and set timetables for the rapture and the "end times". Tim LaHaye and Jerry

Jenkins multimillion-dollar *Left Behind* novels have connected with this fear that the "end" was near and have given to their readers a contorted interpretation of biblical prophecy that has been accepted by millions as the authentic message of the Bible. Rather than getting their theology about the end of the world from preaching, Bible study, hymns and in church settings, millions have received their religious insights from the writers of *Left Behind* fiction. In times of uncertainty many look for clear, simple and certain words of guidance, assurance and confidence. These writers and preachers claim to have a "direct line" to understanding these varied events and how they fit into God's plan and intent for Christians and the rest of humanity. On 60 Minutes, LaHaye said that 9/11 was a "wake up call to America". His books may be fiction, he observed, but they are based on hard facts to help people get ready for Christ's return.

## DOOMSDAY PREACHERS

The writers of the *Left Behind* novels have not been the only voices to speak or write about the "end times". Many American televangelists and futuristic writers have communicated a clear message that all of the recent "significant" events and global catastrophes in our modern world confirm that the predictions from biblical prophecies about the end of the world are speaking about our time in history. The "granddaddy" and founder of this modern dispensational premillennialism view of the Bible was John Nelson Darby, a priest in the Anglican Church of Ireland who died in 1882. He became disillusioned with the Anglican state-church and joined the Plymouth Brethren Church around 1882.[3] According to Dave MacPhersan, Darby's concept of the Rapture was rooted in the vision a young fifteen-year-old girl, named Margaret MacDonald, had in Port Glasgow, Scotland, when she went to a healing service one night in 1830. In this service she had a vision of the return of Christ in two stages. Darby is said to have utilized and expanded on her vision and taught that Jesus would return not just once but twice.[4] Only the Christians who would be "raptured" out of this world to Heaven would experience the first return of Jesus. After a period of seven years of tribulation, Jesus would return a second time in a "Glorious Appearing" and set up his

---

3. Couch, *Dictionary of Premillennial Theology*, 83. See also Walker, *A History of the Christian Church*, 500; and an earlier book, Kraus, *Dispensationalism in America*.

4. MacPherson, *The Rapture Plot*.

kingdom in this world. Followers of Darby like Tim LaHaye, Gerald B. Stanton, John Walvoord, Thomas Ice and others deny that Darby's vision was drawn from MacDonald's visions, but that it "virtually jumped out of the pages of Scriptures once he accepted and consistently maintained the distinction between Israel and the church."[5] John F. Walvoord, former President of Dallas Theological Seminary, and one of the foremost advocates of the pretribulation view and whose teachings and books had a great influence on Tim LaHaye and other fundamentalists, wrote a book entitled *The Rapture Question* which was first published in 1957 and went into the eighteenth printing in the November 1978 printing, claiming 60,000 copies in print.[6]

The order of things that God has arranged on the earth, Darby called a "dispensation." When a group fails to fulfill its responsibility given by God, judgment comes and dispensation ends. Darby saw seven dispensations or ages in the world order.[7] The Bible nowhere speaks of these seven "ages." Darby read this into the text. According to him, the present age is the sixth dispensation, which began with the death of Christ. In Darby's view the world would continue to get worse until the true believers in Christ would be raptured, taken from the earth into Heaven, and then the Antichrist would come and seven years of awful tribulation would begin. A small group of persons would turn to Christ in belief, the remnant, during the tribulation, and they would survive until after the Battle of Armageddon when Christ returned and set up his thousand-year reign. Darby believed that the church had become weak and worldly and had declined in its spirituality "exactly in proportion as the doctrine of the expectation of the Savior's return had been lost sight of."[8] In his seven trips to the United States, Darby led many to adopt his new interpretation of the Scriptures. His theology underwrites much of the fundamentalist thinking today about eschatology, the study of the last days, and their writings, both fictional and nonfiction. LaHaye devotes a chapter with arguments from several "researchers" to affirm that Darby "drew his views primarily from his study of the Word of God, the inspiration of the Holy Spirit and the influence of emerging premillennial biblical literalists, who

5. LaHaye, *The Rapture*, 183.
6. Walvoord, *The Rapture of the Church*. See also a later book by Walvoord, *End Times*.
7. Couch, *Dictionary of Premillennical Theology*, 84.
8. Darby, *The Hopes of the Church of God*, 24.

were moving from the Historical school of interpreting prophecy to the Futurist position."⁹

Darby traveled several times to the United States and persuaded many with his teachings. One of his prominent disciples was Cyrus I. Scofield, Congregational/Presbyterian minister, who published the *Scofield Reference Bible* in 1909. Drawing on Darby's system of dispensation, Scofield added heading and notes in the margin of the Bible, which set forth his fundamentalist view of the biblical passages. Scofield's version of the *King James Version of the Bible* was purchased by millions of people who often saw his interpretations and listings on the same level as Scripture. The *Scofield Reference Bible* was clearly one of the most powerful instruments for ushering in the familiarity with dispensation theology in the United States. Two million people bought the 1967 edition of the *Scofield Reference Bible* which promised to Christian believers that they would rise with the resurrected dead in the clouds with Jesus (the Rapture) and the unbelievers left would suffer seven years of the tribulations of plagues, pestilence, earthquakes, fires, floods and wars as punishment for their sins and unbelief. The Chinese army would destroy half of those who survived the other torments. Worse punishments come upon the unbelievers when the Antichrist (Satan) appears, but he is ultimately destroyed with the unbelievers in the lake of fire (hell) and the old earth is destroyed and a new heaven and earth arises. All this is according to the *Scofield Bible* in keeping with biblical prophecy.

The publication of the *Late Great Planet Earth* in 1970 by Hal Lindsey brought a renewed emphasis on Darby's dispensational system of belief. *The New York Times* recognized Lindsey's book as the top selling nonfiction book of the 1970's. Thomas Ice states that the *Late Great Planet Earth* "becomes the greatest selling book in the history of Christendom next to the Bible itself."[10] Lindsay's book introduced many newcomers to the Christian faith and especially the dispensational premillennialism interpretation of the Bible. Educated at Dallas Seminary, Lindsay's views seemed to have been influenced by his pastor, Robert Thieme, and the lectures of Merrill F. Unger.[11] Lindsey's successful book soon merited him the distinction as the leading prophecy teacher of his day. He connected

---

9. LaHaye, *The Rapture*, 187.

10. Couch, *Dictionary of Premillennical Theology*, 242.

11. MacPherson, *The Three R's*, 109–14. See also "The Lindsey Legend," in MacPherson, *The Incredible Cover-Up*, 131–37.

the fears many had of nuclear holocaust and Russia with biblical prophecy. He taught that within a generation (forty years) after Israel was established as a nation in 1948, the Lord would return.[12] When the Lord did not return in 1988 and the Soviet Union collapsed in the 1990's, Lindsey removed and "corrected" his former interpretations in subsequent editions of *The Late Great Planet Earth*. In new editions of his famous book and recent publications, such as *The Rapture: Truth or Consequences* and *Planet Earth—2000 A.D.: Will Mankind Survive?*, Lindsey predicts that the former Soviet southern republics, which are mostly Muslim, will join with other Islamic forces in the Middle East to attack Israel. Drawing on the contemporary world problems of AIDS, drugs, crime, ethnic cleansing, natural disasters, pseudo religion, immorality, etc., Lindsey still predicts that we are living in the last days, which are within the lifetime of those who are living today.[13]

Several televangelists like Jack Van Impe, Jerry Falwell and Pat Robertson have predicted the end was near and have fanned the dangerous fiery embers of the fear of many. Van Impe wrote that China would be the nation the Bible predicts that would wage war against Israel in the Battle of Armageddon before Jesus returns and sets up his thousand year earthly reign. He "foresaw" that somewhere around the year 2000, the movement toward the last days was to begin.[14] Both Jerry Falwell and Pat Robertson have stated that they believe that AIDS, nuclear war and the worldwide pollution problems are representative of the "plagues" which are unleashed by the Seven Seals in the Book of Revelation. They have both predicted that the end was near but have backed away from their prediction of the timetable when it was not politically expedient.

Pat Robertson states that droughts, forest fires, floods, terrorism and many other signs are warnings that something worse is coming. "Time is running out. No doubt at some point God will say 'Enough!' The only question is when?"[15] Jim Baker, another former televangelist, declared, "a few important prophecies have yet to be fulfilled, but by all appearances

---

12. Lindsey, *Late Great Planet Earth*, 43.
13. Lindsey, *Planet Earth*, 12, 22–26.
14. Van Impe, *2001*, 198–99.
15. Robertson, *Bring It On*, 294.

their potential fulfillment is imminent."[16] John Hagee is even more certain. "The end is near. Without a doubt, we are the terminal generation."[17]

## MILLENNIAL MADNESS

As the calendar approached the year 2000, every radio and television station had special programs reflecting on this momentous occasion. Magazines such as *Time* and *Newsweek* had special issues that listed the important events, persons, inventions, discoveries, scientific, technological and medical breakthroughs, writings, music, art, etc. for the last thousand years and predications from various persons on what the next century would be like. Various theologians and preachers have pointed backward and forward to lessons we can learn from our past millennium that might guide us into the new century. Others saw the coming of a new millennium as a sign of the imminent return of Christ. The word millennium is the word Christians use to depict the thousand-year reign of Christ after he returns to set up his kingdom on earth as denoted in Revelation 20:1–10.

The reference to the millennium in the Book of Revelation is the only place it is mentioned in the New Testament. Nevertheless, the impact of this biblical image has reached far beyond religious circles and has left its mark on the rest of society as well. The writer of Revelation drew from Jewish apocalyptic literature to describe the kingdom of a thousand years that Christ would establish when he returned. Allusions can be traced to the *Book of Daniel, Ezekiel* 38–29, *Isaiah* 24–27 and non-biblical sources like *II Enoch* 32–33, the *Apocalypse of Elijah* and others. Much controversy and division have surrounded this word. This concept will be examined more closely in a later chapter.

With the approach of the new millennium in 2000, some new prophets of gloom arose on the horizon and have warned that we were going to face dire problems in the new century. Some of these concerns focused around the "millennium bug" or the Y2K problem. Stated simply, this problem centered on the fact that when computers were first built they had limited storage space or memory to contain all four digits of a calendar year. Computers had only two digits for a year instead of four. For example, a computer did not store "1999." It only stored "99." Many

---

16. Baker, *Prosperity and the Coming Apocalypse*, 115.
17. Hagee, *Final Dawn Over Jerusalem*, 182.

feared that, when the year 2000 came, computers, if they were not compliant, would not recognize the year "2000" and read only "00". Michael S. Hyatt, author of a New York Times Bestseller, *The Millennium Bug-How to Survive the Coming Chaos*, published in 1998, stated that the "millennium bug" was a digital time bomb that could cause a giant hard disc failure. Unless they were repaired or replaced, Hyatt believed that every microcomputer, mainline computer and imbedded chip system would be affected.

With the arrival of the new century, others predicted that the United States and other countries in the world would have electrical shutdowns, meltdowns, blackouts, brownouts and many other problems because many cities and regions had not prepared for the "millennium bug." Others predicted that there would be worldwide water problems and food shortages. Others said that banks would fail and there would be global recession and financial problems around the world. Others stated that hospitals might not be able to function properly, pharmaceutical supplies might not be rendered correctly, airplanes might crash because of computer failure, and airports would probably not be able to function suitably. Some banks spent as much as eight billion dollars to make their computers compliant. Many banks feared that there would be a mass rush by customers to withdraw money as the millennium approached. Many banks had prepared to have on hand two hundred billion dollars for customers who wanted to take their money from the bank. According to an Associated Press poll in July 7, 1999, one-quarter of the population were going to take extra money out of the bank as the year 2000 approached.

Millennium fears caused many persons to store up extra clothing, water and food, purchase a generator, get all kinds of batteries and some even built a "safe" hiding place. Some dishonest persons used the Y2K fears to try to steal money from people by telling them their money was not safe in their present bank but, if they would transfer their money into the caller's "special account", they would be assured of its security. Some unsuspecting persons were caught in this scam.

Many doomsday preachers envisioned the millennium as a "time—sign" that the end of the world was near and maybe the beginning of the millennium would mark the time of the second coming of Christ. The Rapture was one of the central focuses of many prophecy preachers.[18] Jack

---

18. For example: Lindsey, *Planet Earth* and *The Rapture*.

Van Impe, for example, produced a video entitled, Left Behind. This video was for the unbelievers who were not taken in the Rapture. In this video Van Impe offered guidelines for unbelievers about what they must do to be saved before the second glorious appearing of Christ.[19] Some like the Heaven's Gate cult believed that the rapture for them was to carry them to a spaceship behind the Hale Bopp comet whose appearance indicated to the believers that the time had arrived to lay down their "vehicles" by committing suicide so they might go to their heavenly home. Signs of approaching gloom, comets, sightings of UFO's, terrorists attacks, natural disasters and other signs, as the third millennium arrived, all pointed for the prophecy evangelists to the reality that we were indeed living in the Last Days.

Jack Van Impe notes that the appearance of four UFO's on a screen in Belgium were a sure sign that "the end is near. Without a doubt, we are the terminal generation." Writing in his book, *Are We Living in the End Times?*, LaHaye observes that Jesus may tarry for one more day, which in his economy is a thousand years, but he goes on to insist that "we have more reason than any generation before us to believe He will come in our generation."[20] A *Time* magazine reporter observed in 1997: "As predicted, the approach of the year 2000 is coaxing all the crazed out of the woodwork. They bring with them a twitchy hybrid of spirituality and pop obsession, part Christian, part Asian mystic, part Gnostic, part X Files . . . we have seen the Beast of the Apocalypse."[21] This picture is a graphic description of the *Left Behind* novels. They are like a mongrel filled with many mixed images, some drawn from science fiction, adventure movies and literal depictions of symbolic figures from the Scriptures to show that the end of the world has really arrived.

## NATURE OUT OF CONTROL

Another factor causing many to think that we are living in the last days is the environmental problems and natural disasters. The occurrence of massive earthquakes, hurricanes, fires floods and other natural phenomena raise questions in the minds of many about whether the world will

---

19. The Van Impe magazine, *Perhaps Today* (May/June, 1996) advertised their *Left Behind* video.

20. LaHaye and Jenkins, *Are We Living in the End Times?*, xi.

21. Lacayo, "The Lure of the Cult?" 45.

survive. Doomsday preachers and writers often use these happenings as evidence that the end is near.

Prophecy evangelists joined with some strange new prophets who appeared on the scene several generations ago and began to predict the end of the world, at least an end to the quality of life, as we know it and likely an end to the planet itself in the not too distant future. These new prophets were not religious leaders but men and women of an emerging science called ecology. Ecology in the broader sense is a study of the environment. This science examines the cause and effect actions of different kinds of life and their surroundings, and the utter dependency those systems have upon each other if the balance of nature is to be maintained. Ecologists are warning that there is a strong link between population, productivity and pollution. They have observed that technology has dug deeply into the natural resources to meet the demands of an ever-increasing population, and humanity has been very much a prodigal with the garbage left over from its "horn of plenty". Barry Commoner, a microbiologist, admonished that the price of pollution could cost humanity its existence. Other than nuclear disaster and terrorism today, people fear mostly the pollution of rivers and the water and what is happening to the ozone layer.[22] The World Wildlife Fund stated in its regular *Living Planet Report* that we are spending nature's capital faster than it can regenerate. "Humanity's reliance on fossil fuels, the spread of cities, the destruction of natural habitats for farmland, and over-exploitation of the oceans," Claude Martin writes in this report, "are destroying Earth's ability to sustain life."[23]

These ecological prophets have shouted loudly that the environmental crisis is apparent on every hand. Our smoke stacks spew into the air each year 2.7 billion pounds of aerial garbage, composed of peroxyacly nitrate, sulfur dioxide, fly ash, asbestos particulates and countless other noxious ingredients.[24] We are able to live on the earth because of the thin layer of atmosphere near the earth's surface. Industry and automobiles have filled the air with chemical pollution that, if not corrected, will de-

---

22. Primavesi, *From Apocalypse to Genesis*, 7.

23. Fowler, "Plundered Planet." See also "A Scary Diagnosis for Planet Earth," B8; Carson, *Silent Spring*; Burdick, *Out of Eden*.

24. Scherff *The Mother Earth Handbook*, 103. See also Brown, *Plan B 2.0*, especially 211, 224, 216, 106–9; Davis, *When Smoke Ran Like Water*; Harrison and Pearce, *AAAS Atlas of Pollution and Environment*; Kerry and Kerry, *This Moment on Earth*; Wilson, *The Creation*.

stroy our air. Industrial waste and raw sewage have poured into our rivers, lakes and oceans and have caused unbelievable damage. In many places people can no longer eat the fish they catch. In some streams and along some shore lines, the fish and oysters are not edible. The EPA projected that 70 to 80 billion dollars needs to be spent to meet the sewage needs of future population growth to protect the waters.[25] Our country spends almost as much money on garbage and waste as we do on the space program, yet it is not nearly enough to solve this growing problem.

These prophets also warned that acid rain is destroying our trees and the excessive logging of the rain forests in the Amazon and Brazil is creating drought and famine in that part of the world. Our ozone layer is being depleted, our polar ice caps are melting, and global warming is a serious threat.[26] The evidence is clearly in now of the impact of global warming on our world. In 2005 The National Academy of Science issued a statement, joining with the science academies of Britain, China, Germany, Japan and other countries, that "there is now evidence that significant global warming is occurring."[27] Sir John Houghton, who has served as Professor of Atmospheric Physics at the University of Oxford, England, founder of the Hadley Centre and editor of the first three reports from the United Nations Intergovernmental Panel on Climate Change, is the foremost spokesperson on global warming. In his monumental book, *Global Warming: The Complete Briefing*, Houghton has warned the world about the dangerous climate changes and calls on all persons to remember that humanity has the responsibility of being good stewards of the earth.[28] In May of 2006 a coordinating agency for global warning research, appointed by the Bush administration that has consistently opposed the view of global warming, concluded that there is "clear evidence of human influences on the climate system."[29]

Al Gore, former Vice-President of the United States, has become one of the new prophets who warn that global warming "is a moral, ethical and spiritual challenge."[30] He believes the scientific evidence is in to alert

---

25. Scherff, 129.

26. Weart, *The Discovery of Global Warming*.

27. Easterbrook, "Finally Feeling the Heat of Global Warming," 12. See also Hotz, "Science on the Front Lines," 17.

28. Houghton, *Global Warming*.

29. Ibid. See also Knupp and Horn, *Earth* and Maslin, *Global Warming*.

30. Gore, *An Inconvenient Truth*, 11.

us to see that the survival of our civilization and the habitability of the earth are at stake. Quoting the leading scientific community, forty-eight of whom are Nobel Prize Winners, Gore notes that "unless we act boldly and quickly to deal with the underlying causes of global warming, our world will undergo a string of terrible catastrophes."[31] On *Larry King Live* recently, Gore said that we probably had only about ten years to try to confront the crisis.[32] Unfortunately, he observes, some of our political leaders have tried to silence and distort the scientific voice and plant skepticism about their warning.[33] Our children will wonder later, Gore asserts, why we chose not to act when we had the opportunity. In his book and in a film with the same name as his book, *An Inconvenient Truth*, Gore is raising his prophetic voice to call our attention to this global threat. Gore himself was awarded the 2007 Nobel Peace Prize for his efforts to alert the world about global warming.

On July 16, 2006, Tom Brokaw narrated a program on the Discovery Channel entitled: "Global Warming: What You Need to Know", produced in alliance with the Discovery Channel, NBC News Production and the BBC. In this two hour special, Brokaw talked with an international group of scientific experts, including Dr. James Hansen, a climate specialist and Princeton Professor, Dr. Michael Oppenheimer, about the melting ice caps and the rising temperatures around the world and the dangers this poses if conditions do not change. Bill McKibben, in an article published in *The Christian Century*, asserts that the environmental crisis in the world today "is at least as morally urgent as the civil rights movement-- maybe even more so, since this is a ruthlessly timed issue. Get the right answer fast, or don't bother."[34] He concludes by observing, "The fuss over creationism seems mighty unimportant, for instance, when you stop to consider what a blasphemous decreation we're engaged in."[35]

The over use of chemical insecticide such as DDT has already spread poisons, which have affected the balance of nature on land, water and in the air. The food we eat, the water we drink, and the air we breathe now have greater risks of cancer and other diseases. Other ecologists,

31. Ibid.
32. Al Gore in an interview on *Larry King Live*, June 18, 2006.
33. Gore, *An Inconvenient Truth*, 268f, 284ff. See also Gore's chapter, "The Carbon Crisis," in his book, *The Assault on Reason*, 191–219.
34. McKibben, "Hot and Bothered," 31.
35. Ibid. See also Copeland, et al., *Antarctica*.

like Paul Ehrlich, believe that soon the earth will reach its limit on the number of people it can sustain. After that population figure is reached, he predicts that millions of people will starve.[36] The warnings by these ecological scientists and the awful images of nature often out of control in its destructive path have added to the agenda of doomsday evangelists that we are approaching or are now living in the last days. Jimmy Carter, former president, has declared that "America is by far the world's leading polluter" and has "departed from its historic bipartisan protection of the global environment" and he calls us back to our responsibility for proper stewardship of God's world.[37]

Ministers, priests and theologians have lifted their voices to face the challenge of how to be good stewards of God's world and how to live in harmony with nature and not be in discord with it. The following are only a few examples of many who have raised their voices to save God's creation: Tony Campolo, Dennis Edwards, Frederick Elder, Eric Rust, Francis A. Schaeffer, John B. Cobb, Jr., Eugene C. Hargrove, and others.[38] But too few in the religious, secular or political world have heeded their urgent plea to date and dangers still exist and the threat of extinction remains real. Many have also noted the connection of the environmental crisis with the world wide problems of racism and injustice. Robert Bullard has addressed these issues in two books he has edited entitled *Unequal Protection* and *The Quest for Environmental Justice*.[39] Bjorn Lamborg has edited a book entitled *Global Crises, Global Solutions* in which he addresses the ten most serious challenges facing the world, such as climate change, communicable diseases, malnutrition and hunger , clean water, etc., and offers constructive approaches to these problems.[40] Hopefully, the political and religious leaders of the world, especially our own gov-

---

36. Ehrlich, *The Population Bomb*, 18ff.

37. Carter, *Our Endangered Values*, 177. See also Gore, *Earth in the Balance*.

38. Campolo, *How to Rescue the Earth*; Edwards, *Jesus and the Cosmos*; Elder, *Crisis in Eden*; Eric C. Rust, *Nature*; Schaefer, *Pollution and the Death of Man*; Birch and Cobb Jr., *The Liberation of Life*; Hargrove, *Beyond Spaceship Earth*; Cobb Jr., *Is It Too Late?*; Hargrove, *Foundations of Environmental Ethics*.

39. Bullard, *Unequal Protection* and *The Quest for Environmental Justice*; McKibben, *The End of Nature*. (McKibben argues that the survival of the globe is dependent on a fundamental, philosophical shift in the way we relate to nature).

40. Lamborg, *Global Crises*.

ernment, will heed the warning and respond appropriately to these crises. The prophetic voices have sounded the alarm!

## AN INTERESTING READ

Although some may not consider the *Left Behind* novels great literature, they are easy to read and they capture the interest of most readers from the beginning and challenge him or her to travel further with the characters in the story. After the first novel or so, the story begins to sound like the adventures of persons behind enemy lines, fighting and scheming to avoid and outwit the powerful world leader, Nicolae Carpathia, whom the believers know is the antichrist. The plots often sound like a snippet, as I mentioned before, from "Mission Impossible" or an adventure from a Tom Clancy novel with the Tribulation Force rescuing someone behind enemy lines or listening to the enemy forces on the hidden bug on Carpathia's own plane or overhearing the plans being made in Global Community Headquarters in New Babylon over the elaborate listening devices and computers that the Tribulation Force's "mole", Chang Wong, has planted and are never discovered. The novels are filled with certain characters having expert knowledge and the use of the best of advanced technology. They travel in Range Rovers, 747's, helicopters and use encryption technology so as not to be detected and each has a high-security satellite phone to communicate with each other.

High adventure carries the Tribulation Force from one city and continent to another. They protect themselves with Uzis, DEWs (a Directed Energy Weapon) or at least lugers. They pray and thank God for his protection as they pack the ammunition they need. The novels are filled with battles, murders, explosions, violence, executions, torture, intrigue, car and plane chases, blood, daring escapes, war, natural disasters, risks, hazards and perils that few could imagine. The thrilling adventures carry the reader to a dramatic conclusion and often keep them suspended until the next novel in the series was published, like the old Saturday matinee serials that left the viewer hanging not knowing if the hero would survive until the segment was seen the next week. There is also a "soap opera" dimension to the novels in the romantic excursions of Rayford Steele, Hattie Durham, Chloe Steele, Buck Williams, Chang Wong, Naomi Tiberius and others.

At times the novels read like horror stories or science fiction. Carpathia puts a spell on all those assembled in the conference room at the United Nation's Building when he calls them to meet after being named Secretary General of the United Nations. Some magical/wizard like trance makes all those in the room, except Buck, whose faith sustained him to witness the truth, "see" Jonathan Stonagal kill Todd-Cothran and then shoot himself. Carpathia actually killed them both to get rid of them, and put everyone under a hypnotic spell or a "mind control" so those present saw only what he wanted them to see. The depictions of the various plagues in the Book of Revelation that arise from the trumpet the angel blows during the days of tribulation strike horror and fear in the mind of the reader. The images, especially of the locusts and 200 million horsemen of the plagues, make Stephen King, Albert Hitchcock, Ray Bradbury or J. K. Rowling look tame.

Many like, for example, the sensational twist LaHaye and Jenkins have given to Ezekiel 38 and 39 where they put jet planes, missiles and atomic weapons along side spears and horses from ancient times in the hands of Carpathia's army for the Battle of Armageddon. The wedding of the supernatural and the sensational, romance and adventure, superior technology and angelic protection, terrifying villains and the power of evil, the Word of God and determined Christian heroes make exciting reading. The novels are captivating in their allurement to entice the reader to come back to the fountain of entertainment for another drink and then another.

Some believers may be drawn to these novels out of a need for the sensational, dramatic and supernatural to confirm that their faith is real. Some have a difficult time separating worship and entertainment, religion and magic, belief and certainty, truth and make believe. Faith for many must be sensational or it seems weak and insipid to them. The strong, military take charge, adventuresome Christian in the Tribulation Force in the *Left Behind* novels are the images many want the Christian to be. The concept of ministry seems far removed from these militant heroes. Many persons today find religion and church dull and uninteresting. These novels are exciting and provocative in the depiction of religion, and many hunger for that and are drawn to the message in this series. These novels also print black and white pictures about good and evil, belief and unbelief, and the natural and supernatural. The Book of Revelation is interpreted literally, mystery and symbolism are divested and the strange book of the Apocalypse is given one clear interpretation that many long for. If faith is described as a simple response, the mystery and concept of a continuously or evolving faith may be ignored. Paul reminds us that we always "see in a mirror dimly" (1 Cor. 13:12 RSV). Too many long for certainty in religion and not for faith. Faith is a commitment of trust in Christ and his way, and we walk in the light of his presence as we sense it through prayer, the Scriptures, the Church, and the Christian witness of the ages. None of us dares to say that he or she has *the* only understanding and interpretation of the Christian faith. We should always remain open for new insights in how to love and serve our Lord.

3

# Left Behind Biblical Terminology

As a boy, I remember riding through the mountains of Virginia and seeing words painted in large, white letters on rocks, which announced boldly, "JESUS IS COMING SOON". I used to wonder to myself, "How do they know?" and "How soon?" Many end times prophets are making that same proclamation today. Tim LaHaye and Jerry Jenkins' *Left Behind* fiction series has attempted to answer those questions and others by telling how Jesus returned secretly to earth and took all the believers with him to Heaven. Those "left behind" are consigned to face seven years of tribulation and whether or not they will respond to the gospel message before Jesus comes again in his Glorious Appearing. LaHaye believes that Jesus will make a secret first return and take the believers from the earth in the "twinkling of an eye". This event is called the Rapture.

Because of the disappearance of Christians, LaHaye asserts that the world will be thrown into panic and chaos as drivers and pilots are snatched out of their cars or planes, which will cause many of the vehicles to crash, and multitudes will be killed. People will be left wondering what has happened to family members and friends who have vanished. Almost every family in many parts of the world will have loved ones disappear, and they will be unable to explain why. The *Left Behind* novels, sixteen in all counting the prequels, tell what happens to certain individuals, like Rayford Steele, a former 747 airline captain for Pan-Continental, his daughter, Chloe, Buck Williams, who becomes Chloe's husband, and others who touched these main character's lives. The novels trace their survival through the seven years of the tribulation, their encounter with the Antichrist and his forces and the Battle of Armageddon until the Glorious Appearing of Jesus.

Behind and throughout these novels, LaHaye and Jenkins exposed a stated view of the Bible, what is called a "dispensational premillennial theology." LaHaye states that the idea about writing the novels came to him when he was flying one day. LaHaye basically outlines the broad prophetic themes of each book, while Jerry Jenkins actually does the writing. Although the writers do draw deeply from the "well" of traditional dispensationalism, they have without question modified it to a degree and added a different perspective on how one understands the "modern" evangelical Christian. Sometimes it is hard to see the real difference between the Rayford Steele before the Rapture and the one after his conversion. He still struggles with many of his old vices—sex, power, wealth, the desire to kill, fits of anger and overt worldliness.

## FACTS BEHIND THE FICTION

This chapter will seek to detail the biblical and theological presuppositions underlying the *Left Behind* novels. This will be done throughout the book not only by examining excerpts from the novels, but examples will also be drawn from some of the non-fiction writings from LaHaye and other dispensationalists as well. The reader needs to be aware that there are other theological and hermeneutical approaches to end time themes that will be discussed in the next chapter. LaHaye has boldly declared that "the *Left Behind* books may be fiction but they are based on hard facts."[1] On the back cover of LaHaye's revised edition of *Revelation Unveiled*, republished in 1999, is the statement that this book is "the biblical foundations for the bestselling *Left Behind* series."[2] Without question, LaHaye believes that his views of the end times are the correct ones and other viewpoints are often dismissed as coming from deceivers or false teachers. His books on basic Bible prophecy and the study of future things will not only give guidance to the readers to understand prophecy better, he maintains, but will equip them to answer these "false teachers who are popping up everywhere."[3]

## THE RAPTURE

The central theological premise for the *Left Behind* novels is the concept of the Rapture. For most people the first thoughts that come to your mind when you hear the word, rapture, are those of ecstasy, bliss, ravishment,

---

1. Tim LaHaye, an interview on *60 Minutes*, February 8, 2004.
2. LaHaye, *Revelation Unveiled*, backcover.
3. LaHaye, *Understanding Bible Prophecy for Yourself*, 9.

great happiness, enthusiasm or delight, not some picture of the end times. The word rapture however has been given a new twist by prophecy teachers. It also does not occur in any English Bibles. It was translated in the Latin Vulgate, produced by Jerome in the early 400s. The Vulgate was the Bible used by the Western church until the time of the Reformation. The Roman Catholic Church still uses it today as its basic Latin translation of the Bible. The one verse that contains the word rapture is found in 1 Thessalonians 4:17 and is usually translated from the Greek "shall be caught up together" or "snatched or seized suddenly". This Greek verb was rendered rapture in Latin that could be translated as "seize, snatch or tear away." The English word rapture, it is evident, is derived from the Latin word. LaHaye uses the Latinized version, *Rapture*, to depict the sudden, secret, surprising return of Christ to take up (rapture) the believers to Heaven. The three main biblical passages that LaHaye and others use to support their concept of the Rapture are John 14:1-3; 1Corinthians 15:50-57; and 1 Thessalonians 4:13-18.

LaHaye believes that the Second Coming of Jesus is mentioned 318 times in the New Testament. At times, he notes in an earlier book, the passages seem to have conflicting concepts. In 1 Thessalonians 4:17 it states that Christ will come "in the air," yet in another passage it is observed that he is coming "to the earth" (Rev 19:19). In one passage, we are taught that at his return, "every eye will see him" (Rev 1:7). Another passages notes that his coming will be in secret "as a thief" (1 Thess. 5:2). One passage predicts that his coming will be a time of joy (Titus 2:13), while another declares that the people on earth will "mourn" (Matt 24:30). LaHaye believes that the only way to explain these seeming conflicts is that there are *two* comings of Jesus. The first one is the Rapture in which Christ will come in secret to take his Christian Church to be with him. This will be a time of joy for the Christians. The Second Coming will be Christ's Glorious Appearing when he will bring joy to the new believers after the first rapture but it will be a time of sorrow for the wicked when he returns to destroy them the second time.[4]

LaHaye has given elaborate schemes and diagrams to demonstrate that the Bible teaches two distinct returns of Christ. The first coming is called the Rapture and the Second Coming is entitled the Glorious Appearing. To prove his theory he lists twenty-three scripture passages

---

4. LaHaye, *The Beginning of the End*, 21. See also the "Author's Note" at the end of LaHaye and Jenkins, *The Rapture*, 348f.

for the Rapture and the same number, although different selections for the Second Coming. He also notes fifteen differences between the Rapture and the Glorious Appearing. In the Rapture or Blessed Hope as he sometimes calls this first coming, Christ will return in the air for his followers. All believers are raptured; they are taken to his Father's house; there is no judgment on the earth; the Church is taken to heaven; this return is imminent; no signs are given, it is for believers only; it is a time of joy; it occurs before the "Day of Wrath"—the tribulation; there is the marriage of the Lamb; only believers will see Christ, and the tribulation begins.[5]

## THE GLORIOUS APPEARING

On the other hand, LaHaye notes the following differences in the Second Coming which he calls the Glorious Appearing: Christ will return to the earth with his believers who were taken in the Rapture and died before that event; no one will be raptured; resurrected Christians do not see the Father's house; Christ will judge all persons on earth; Christ sets up his Kingdom on earth; this appearing will not occur for at least seven years; there will be many signs of Christ's physical coming; it will affect all of humanity; it will be a time of mourning and come right after the tribulation. Satan will be bound for a thousand years; there will be no time or place for a judgment seat; Christ's bride, the Church, will descend with him; everyone will see him; and Christ's thousand-year reign will begin.[6]

The Glorious Appearing, which is also the name of the twelfth novel in the series, will be the stellar event that triggers the Millennium, the thousand-year reign of Christ on earth. This appearing has also been called "The Coming of the Son of Man," "The second advent," "the revelation" or "the second coming." In this coming Christ will not be seen as the Suffering Servant but as a reigning Lord who will be worshipped by human beings and angels. This coming will conclude God's involvement with humanity for six thousand years since He created Adam and Eve and placed them in the Garden of Eden. The world, according to LaHaye and other dispensationalists is literally only six thousand years old. The thousand-year reign of Christ during the Millennium will complete earth's history of seven thousand years. The Glorious Appearing will bring an

---

5. LaHaye, *Understanding Bible Prophecy for Yourself,* 46–47.
6. Ibid., 47.

end to sin, injustice and all the brutality and hard-heartedness that have existed in the world. It will be the world's greatest event.[7]

Much of what is evidenced in LaHaye's distinction between the two comings is clearly spelled out and dramatically treated in the twelve volume *Left Behind* series. LaHaye's interpretation falls neatly into the premillennial view of the Bible. His particular understanding of the Bible is the one expounded throughout his novels. Too many readers assume that the view in the novels is *the* only way or, as LaHaye likes to say, the only way to understand correctly the Bible. But as I will show in the next chapter, there are many other ways to interpret the Bible and end times' prophecy. LaHaye's view is actually a minority view and held by only a few scholars. To read the book of Revelation and many other passages about the Second Coming literally, not only is a misreading of the text but also is a distortion of the meaning and purpose that lay behind the original biblical writer's intention. On the other hand, since no New Testament text ever says "Second Coming," the whole notion of the Rapture is a figurative or speculative interpretation. In addition, finding tanks and helicopters in Revelation is an imaginative and not a literal reading. LaHaye has arbitrarily used many poetic, symbolic, metaphorical, and visionary images, themes and ideas and actually missed the reasons the ancient writer had for using them in the first place to communicate to the persons to whom they were primarily addressed. He and Jenkins have created captivating stories, but many of them bordering on the science fiction level and, I believe, lead to a distorted image of the Bible and of God.

These two distinct comings of Christ, according to LaHaye, will be separated by a seven-year interval called the tribulation. As I mentioned earlier, LaHaye draws his belief in seven years as a fulfillment of the prophecy in Daniel about the "seventieth week" (Dan. 9:24–27). This concept is called "the pretribulation view" of Christ's return. The use of the prefix, "*pre*", denotes that the Rapture occurs before the seven years of tribulation. If the Prefix, "*post*", was added, this would designate that the Rapture would follow the period of Tribulation. LaHaye is a strong advocate of the pretribulation view.[8]

---

7. LaHaye, *The Rapture*, 88–89.
8. LaHaye, *The Beginning of the End*, 21ff.

## DISPENSATIONALISM

Another foundational stone in LaHaye's theology is his dispensationalism. He follows Darby in his central themes. Dispensationalism is sort of like a philosophy of history which divides history into seven successive areas, epochs or, if you please, dispensations. The seven dispensations are called innocence, conscience, civil government, promise or patriarchal rule, Mosaic Law, grace and the last, the Millennium. Beginning with Adam, history is traced through periods dealing with the flood, the tower of Babel, the patriarchs, the years of Jewish slavery, the giving of the law, salvation by grace and concludes with the thousand-year reign of Christ after his Glorious Second Advent. This system is characterized by stating that the church is distinct from Israel because God has distinct plans for each. Dispensationalists do not believe that the Church is the New Israel or has displaced Israel in the promises God made to that nation. God will literally fulfill these promises to Israel. The reconstitution of Israel as a nation in 1948 was seen as a major sign in the fulfillment of that promise. And the rebuilding of the temple will be another major factor. The Church, the Bride of Christ, will be raptured to Heaven and the seven years of tribulation will begin.[9]

## THE SEVEN-YEAR TRIBULATION

A fundamental tenet in the *Left Behind* series is the view of a seven-year period of tribulation for those who are not raptured. All twelve of these novels are set in this "seven-year" Tribulation period of time except for a few pages in the final novel, *Glorious Appearing*. A lot of pages are constructed around several isolated verses found in the book of Daniel. "Seventy weeks marked out for your people . . . seven weeks will pass . . . then sixty-two weeks and he will make a firm covenant with the many for one week, but in the middle of the week he will put a stop to sacrifice and grain offering" (Dan. 9:24–27). LaHaye interprets these "seven weeks" to symbolize seven years, but it does not literally state that anywhere in that chapter in Daniel. And it is a serious issue to assume that this prophet was talking about a period of time following the Second Coming of Christ. Although the writer of the Book of Revelation uses the number seven more than fifty times, there is no reference to seven years of tribulation.

---

9. Couch, "Dispensationalism," 93–99. See also Witherington, *Revelation*, 260–64.

The end times fiction novels set in a seven year period of tribulation seems to be a fabrication drawn out of LaHaye's imaginative use of Scripture.

LaHaye and other defenders of this view draw also from the words of Jesus in Matthew 24:3–21 where he speaks about the suffering in "a great tribulation "(v. 21). They also like to point to the references to "three and a half years" mentioned in Revelation 11:2, 13:5, for example. They find "ways" to add these two periods together to get their seven years. The central thrust for this concept, however, is drawn from the ninth chapter of Daniel. The term "week' or "sets of weeks," according to these advocates, refers to a period of seven years.

## A LITERAL INTERPRETATION OF SCRIPTURE

A cardinal belief of dispensational theology is their hermeneutics (a way of interpreting the Bible) of taking a literal interpretation of the Scripture. The golden rule of biblical interpretation, according to LaHaye, is "to take every word at its primary, literal meaning unless the facts of the immediate context clearly indicate otherwise."[10] Literalism seeks to discern the actual words and meaning of a text and opposes the allegorical or symbolic use of Scripture. He takes the reference to the antichrist, the two witnesses, the plagues, woes, bowls of wrath, the judgments, Babylon, Armageddon and others in Revelation literally. LaHaye's literal interpretation clearly puts him in the camp of the thorough going dispensationalists. In almost surprising literalism, LaHaye depicts the various happenings as they are prophesized in Revelation. The Tribulation Force witnesses or experiences this fulfillment of prophecies as actual events in their lives as they are played out in these fictional tales. Tsion Ben-Judah, the former rabbinical scholar who became a believer, was the spiritual teacher of more than a billion through cyberspace. He became the chief interpreter of biblical prophecy to those left behind during the Tribulation.

LaHaye, however, did not always stick to his own golden rule of interpretation. In his commentary on Revelation, *Revelation Unveiled*, he gives various examples of why certain things should not be interpreted literally. Look for example at his understanding of Revelation 12:1–2 and 14:4.[11] In the *Glorious Appearing* the sharp sword which comes out of Jesus' mouth to "smite the nations" (Rev 19:5) was not taken literally but

---

10. LaHaye, *The Rapture*, 238. See "Author's Note" in *The Rapture*, 348f.
11. LaHaye, *Revelation Unveiled*, 1999, 202, 228ff.

was interpreted as the quotations of Scripture. The Scripture quotations were the sword that destroyed those who had the mark of the Beast in the final battle of Armageddon. In some places the seas and rivers literally turn to blood while the moon only appears to change. In chapter 6 of Revelation the four horses are interpreted symbolically but Jesus' Glorious Appearing has him literally riding a white horse. Everything in the Scriptures, of course, especially in Revelation, should not be taken literally. But LaHaye has long argued that it should be and yet he does not always follow his own fundamental principle. As will be noted later, the attempt to take most of the Book of Revelation literally likely causes one to miss the basic vision and meaning of the book for its own day and for our day as well.

When readers step into the world of the *Left Behind* novels, they are often puzzled and confused by the many strange and unusual words and images they meet. Even persons who have grown up in church settings are often not familiar with these figures and vocabulary. Let us examine a few of these key words that LaHaye and Jenkins use in their writings. I will begin with what might seem like the obvious. But it might be helpful not to assume, that everyone understands the meaning of all these strange sounding words.

## BEGINNING AT THE END

The word, eschatology, is the theological word used to describe "the study of the last things" or "the study of the end times". It is derived from the Greek word, *eschatos,* which means "last" or "last things". This usually deals with the Christian view of death, resurrection, the Second Coming of Christ, the judgment, Heaven and Hell. Some also include various understandings of the Millennium (discussed later), the End of the Age, the Day of the Lord, the Last Days, and other terms. Eschatology seeks to explain how history will end as it moves toward its final consummation under the Lordship of Christ.

The phrase, "The End Times" is a popular way of speaking about eschatology. End Times is simply a way of describing how the world as we know it will arrive at its final state. In the *Left Behind* series the Tribulation Force, the band of recently converted Christians after the Rapture, often speak of themselves as living in the end times. Prophecy writers frequently describe the age we are now living in as the end times, meaning that history is at the point where Jesus will be coming soon.

In an interview with Larry King on CNN, LaHaye was asked by King, "Do you believe that some sort of end is coming?" "Yes," LaHaye responded and continued, "In fact, I believe there are a number of signs in Scripture that indicate it's going to come pretty soon. We say maybe within our lifetime."[12] LaHaye is convinced that we are living in the last days before Christ returns. "What many people don't realize is just how ripe world conditions are for the end times."[13] Noting that no one knows for certain when Christ will return, LaHaye is bold to assert, "We believe, however, that Christians living today have more reason than those of our generation before us to believe that Christ will come in our lifetime."[14] An article LaHaye contributed to a book focusing on end times bears the title, "Twelve Reasons Why This Could Be The Terminal Generation."[15] LaHaye writes about the end times because he believes we are living in them and that he knows and understands the signs.

## APOCALYPSE

The word *Apocalypse* comes from the Greek term that means "to reveal," "uncover," "disclose" or "lifting of the veil." The Book of Revelation bears the title *Apocalypse* which refers to its unveiling the events to come in the future. The *Book of Revelation* is the main source from which LaHaye and Jenkins draw most of the themes for their novels. The writers often use the term apocalypse to describe catastrophic events that are coming in the end times with the Rapture, the Tribulation and the Battle of Armageddon. Parts of the books of Daniel, Zechariah, Joel, Amos, and Isaiah have been described as apocalyptic literature and are often used by prophecy writers as similar types to the *Apocalypse* or *Revelation*. The *Left Behind* writers draw from some of these sources as well, especially Daniel and Zechariah.

---

12. Larry King Live, CNN on June 19, 2000.
13. LaHaye, *Understanding Bible Prophecy for Yourself*, 215.
14. LaHaye and Jenkins, *Are We Living in the End Times?*, 363.
15. Ice and Demy, *When the Trumpet Sounds*, 429.

## THE MILLENNIUM

Millennium comes from two Latin words, *mille,* "thousand" and *annus,* "year." A Millennium indicates a period of a thousand years. In the Bible, especially in Revelation 20:1–10, it refers to the thousand year reign of Christ after his Second Coming. The primary references to the Millennium in the *Left Behind* series is to the event that will take place after the Glorious Appearing of Christ. The last novel, *Kingdom Come,* presents LaHaye and Jenkin's interpretation of the Millennium. LaHaye believes that this event will be a literal Kingdom over which Christ will rule on earth. He sees it as "the most blessed time this world has known since the Garden of Eden,"[16] but it is not heaven and men and women who are not Christians can still sin.[17]

*Premillennialists,* like LaHaye, believe that Christ comes first in the Rapture, the seven years of Tribulation takes place, and then Christ comes in the Second Coming or the Glorious Appearing. Following the Glorious Appearing, the Millennium—the reign of Christ for a thousand years—will take place. Another group called *Postmillennialist* believes that the Tribulation and Rapture or Second Coming will occur after the thousand year rule of the church on earth while Christ is still in heaven. Still another interpretation is called *amillennial,* which views the Millennium in a symbolic sense. They understand Christ's rule to have begun at his resurrection and they deny any literal future Kingdom of Christ on earth. His Kingdom, according to their view, is spiritual and not literal and is a present reality and not future. Christ's Kingdom is working through the church today.

It has always been interesting to me how many articles, books, and schools of thought have been structured around the Millennium theme, especially since the book of Revelation devotes only three verses to this topic (Rev 20:4–6). It is also not even mentioned anywhere else in the New Testament. Many of these various camps have assumed that they alone have the correct insight into these views and have often divided churches, theological schools and colleges over their interpretations. LaHaye has devoted hundreds of pages in fiction and nonfiction to espouse his pretribulation, dispensational view of the millennium. As a friend of mine once said, "I don't get all the white lipped, tight fisted attitudes about who's right—*pre,*

---

16. LaHaye, *Understanding Biblical Prophecy for Yourself,* 179.
17. LaHaye and Jenkins, *Kingdom Come,* xiii–xiv.

*post* or *a*. I'm a *Panmillennialist*. It's all going to *pan* out in the end, and so I don't worry about it". Only God ultimately knows the future.

## THE ANTICHRIST

In premillennialistic theory the Antichrist is depicted as the final world ruler who will oppose God and Christ. He will claim to be divine and deny the divinity of Christ. He will oppress the Jewish people; God's elect, and will desecrate the Jewish temple and Jerusalem and will seek to usurp the worship that was afforded the holy God for himself.[18]

One of the leading characters in the *Left Behind* series is introduced in the first volume. A warning comes early about a new, charismatic leader who has arisen to guide the world during a time of chaos and confusion. He will make many promises but will break them because he is a great deceiver. This person is predicted in the Bible. He is the Antichrist.[19] In the fiction of LaHaye and Jenkins, Nicolae Jetty Carpathia, in his late thirties and former president of Romania, rises to the world stage to become the "self-appointed Global Community potentate", on a platform of world peace. His intelligence and charm are amazing. He is described as "blonde and blue eye like the original Romanians."[20] According to LaHaye's theology or eschatology, the Antichrist had to be Roman because he interpreted Scripture to show that the antichrist would come out of a reconstituted Roman Empire. Romanians in LaHaye's viewpoint are actually Italian in their heritage.

Nicolae makes a seven-year treaty with Israel and many think that he is the Messiah. At the three-and-a-half year mark, he breaks his treaty with Israel and begins to persecute the Jews and those who have become believers after the Rapture. He calls for everyone to worship him and to bear the mark of loyalty to him or to be put to death. For the final three-and-a-half years of the tribulation, Nicolae, the Antichrist, controls the whole world politically, economically and religiously. Much of the novels are built around the believers—the Tribulation Force—as they come to be called, and their conflict, encounters and survival with the forces and powers of the Antichrist. In these fictional accounts the Antichrist is given a personal identification as Nicolae Jetty Carpathia who has what

---

18. Couch, "AntiChrist," 43.
19. LaHaye and Jenkins, *Left Behind*, 212–13.
20. Ibid., 70.

seems like "divine" or supernatural powers. Even after he was assassinated in Jerusalem, he resurrected himself from his coffin in the Global Community Palace complex in New Babylon before the eyes of millions who witnessed it in person or via television. The Antichrist has been given extraordinary power by Satan to try and counter the miraculous power of Jesus.

Throughout history end time prophets have tried to link the Antichrist with cruel world leaders or anyone that opposed the Christian way or even the democratic government or they might not have liked. Persons like Caligula, Domitian, Montanus, Napoleon, Julius Caesar, Hitler, Stalin, Anwar el Sadet, Sun Myung Moon, Mikhail Gorbachev, many of the popes, Saddam Hussein, and even John Kennedy, Henry Kissinger, Ronald Reagan, Bill Clinton, and many others have made the list. Many have tried to guess the Antichrist's identity and have failed again and again. Time and time again some person has been depicted as the antichrist, and this was always supposed to indicate that the end was near. But every time, the Second Coming did not happen and history moved on to another figure to take his place.

LaHaye believes that at least twenty titles have been given to the Antichrist in the Scriptures. Among these he lists "King of Babylon" (Isa. 7:8, 8:9), "Lucifer" (Isa. 14:2), "little horn" (Dan. 7:8, 8:9), "a stern-face king" (Dan. 8:23), "The ruler who will come" (Dan. 9:26), "Mighty King" (Dan. 11:36), "man of lawlessness" (2 Thess. 2:3–8), "a beast coming out of the sea" (Rev 13:1) and the "antichrist" (1 John 2:18).[21] After the church has been raptured, LaHaye contends, the Antichrist will make his appearance during the seven-year period of Tribulation and demand, after a brief seemingly peaceful time, absolute loyalty from all and the requirement that everyone bear the "mark of the beast". Eventually the Antichrist, according to LaHaye, will lead the world forces loyal to him in a battle against the Christians in the final battle of Armageddon.

Since dualism was a basic concept in apocalypticism, it is not unexpected to find the concept of an Antichrist, a sort of demonic adversary of Christ, who would oppose him in the time of his return. Some scholars have found the roots for this apocalyptic concept in Babylonian or Iranian beliefs. Premillennial writers and preachers focus heavily on this concept of the Antichrist. In the *Dictionary of Premillennial Theology*, edited by

---

21. LaHaye, *Revelation Unveiled*, 207–8.

Mal Couch, ten pages are devoted to various aspects of the Antichrist.[22] Probably the earliest Christian teaching about this view is found in what is called the Little Apocalypse of Mark 13 where Jesus predicts that before he returns again that many false Christs and false prophets will come and deceive many with signs and wonders. Note not just one but many false Christs or Messiahs will challenge the believers. Some see the reference to "the desolating sacrilege" as to an antichrist figure, while others see it as a reference to the desecration of the Jewish temple by some evil tyrant like Emperor Caligula who ordered his statue set up in the Jewish temple which profaned it or as a reference to the desecration of the temple by Antiochus IV Epiphanies. "This passage suggests," according to Pheme Perkins, "that readers should recognize the fulfillment of the prophecy."[23]

Paul, writing in 2 Thessalonians 2:3ff speaks about the "man of lawlessness," this "son of perdition," who takes his seat in the temple and exalts himself as a god before the final return of Christ. The reference to the desecration of the temple again is likely pointing to Caligula or Antiochus IV, and the "man of lawlessness" may be a reference to one of the Roman emperors. But the Antichrist is also one who embodies Satan and is an adversary of Christ in his second advent.[24]

Like other end times prophets who have attempted to force the biblical views about the Antichrist to fit a particular person in history, LaHaye's image makes interesting fictional reading. But he places all the Antichrist references to events which are to happen thousands of years later and are unrelated to the people to whom the ancient Scriptures were written. The only place the word Antichrist is found in the Bible is in two of the Johnannine epistles—1 John 2:18, 22; 4:3; 2 John 7. These passages clearly indicated that the Antichrist is not a particular person but "anyone who denies that Jesus is the Christ" and anyone "who denies the Father and the Son" (1 John 2:22). "Every spirit which does not confess Jesus is not of God. This is the spirit of the Antichrist" (1 John 4:3). John the Elder was engaging the Docetic Christian belief that confessed that Jesus was spirit, but denied that he really became incarnate.

John drew upon the widespread belief in the Antichrist when he observed that "You have heard that Antichrist is coming" and then asserts

22. Couch, "Antichrist," 43–53.
23. Perkins, "The Gospel of Mark," 690.
24. Rist, "Antichrist," 142.

that "many Antichrists have come" (1 John 2:18). His basic purpose in writing his letters was not to try to identify the Antichrist as a particular individual, although he likely held to the ancient belief in an Antichrist figure, but to alert Christians to the reality that *anyone* who denies Christ as Lord incarnate is an Antichrist. He was drawing upon Jesus' warning in Mark 13 about many false Christs that would come to try to deceive the early Christian believers. The Antichrist John writes about is not so much a person as basically a false concept or belief. Any person, who denies the Lordship of Christ, in particular the incarnation, is committing the sin of the Antichrist. False teachers are those who say it doesn't make any difference what you believe about Christ. You may think he was a good person, a great teacher, or a miracle worker but that is not sufficient. The central focus of our faith is the basic creed, "Jesus is Lord". There may be many areas where Christians may differ, but the fundamental, uncompromising belief is the Lordship of Christ, the one who became incarnate as the Son of God. This is the church's earliest and basic confession of faith.

To deny the belief in the incarnation and the Lordship of Christ and propagate a way of life or belief that contradicts Christ's sacrifice and teaching and yet pretend that their belief is the Christian way, like the teachings of the Ku Klux Klan or some other hate group, is heresy or the spirit or manner of the Antichrist. The battle John is describing with the Antichrist takes place within ones' own mind and soul to discern the truth about the nature of Christ (Christology) and respond in a genuine commitment of faith and discipleship and not to acknowledge Christ and then later denying him. Jesus asked his disciples in his day and now asks each person who would follow him the ultimate question which demands an answer of a firm affirmation of faith: "Who do you say that I am?" (Matt 16:15) The Incarnation remains central to our faith. To deny it puts us in the camp of the "many" Antichrists.

The Antichrist may have been perceived by some in ancient times as an "individual", but "most current interpreters are content to view the antichrist as a general embodiment of evil."[25] John in his epistle was denoting that the Antichrist was not just one individual who will arise to tempt and destroy the Church but is one of many who will seek to spread false teachings and lead Christians to commit apostasy. Paul warned the early church to watch out for those who rejected the resurrection of Christ (1

---

25. Myers, "Antichrist," 60.

Cor. 15:12), preached a different gospel (Gal. 1:6–9), or who were false teachers or taught corrupt doctrines (Rom. 16:17–18; Phil. 3:18–19; Acts 20:18–30) and in many other places Peter warned about false prophets (2 Pet. 2:1) and so did John in Revelation 2:2. These are just a few samples of the New Testament's warning about false teachings that deny Jesus as Lord. John stated that "the spirit of the antichrist is already now in the world" (1 John 4:13). It was a present problem in his own day in the first century. John's depiction of the Antichrist was an image of one at work in the world then and was not some vague figure he saw coming many thousands of years later.

Thousands of pages in the *Left Behind* novels are built around the depiction of the Antichrist as an individual person. As long as the readers understand that this is a fictional account and is based on a premillennial interpretation of biblical teachings, then the books make for interesting reading. But to declare that this interpretation is the only solid biblical teaching is questionable and frankly dangerous. For one who claims to take the Scriptures literally, why does LaHaye not also take the clear teaching of 1 John literally in his declaration of the meaning of the Antichrist as *anyone* who denies that Christ is Lord?

## THE BEAST

Another image LaHaye uses for the Antichrist is "a beast coming out of the sea" (Rev 13:1). He sees this figure of the Beast as John's special name for the "godless world leader".[26] In the *Left Behind* fictional accounts, it is Nicolae, "the Antichrist" or "the Beast", who kills the two witnesses to Christ in Jerusalem. The Beast is depicted as the one who blasphemes God and God's Tabernacle (Rev 13:5–7). It is the Beast who demands worship and receives a mortal wound. LaHaye insists that the Beast is actually killed because his wound causes him to descend to the bottomless pit and ascend from there to the earth when he is resurrected. He sees this as a sort of counterfeit image of Christ's death and resurrection. This resurrection will be "the marvel" that will cause millions to worship him.[27]

In chapter 13 of Revelation there are two beasts, one that arises from the sea (Rev 13:1–10) and another that is a beast that comes out of the earth (Rev 13:11–18). Most biblical scholars identify "the Beast from the

---

26. LaHaye and Jenkins, *Are We Living In the End Times?*, 279.
27. Ibid., 281.

sea" in Revelation 13 with the Roman Empire and its embodiment of evil and oppression in the emperors.[28] The "beast from the earth" is most likely, according to David E. Aune and George Beasley-Murray, representative of the "imperial priesthood, which was centrally concerned with promoting the imperial cult."[29] Both images are likely referring to all the evil and horrors which had come from the seven Roman emperors. Kenneth H. Maaks sees the second beast as "a split personality" of the other one from the sea John describes in the first part of the chapter.[30]

The person most likely fitting that image and who was the one persecuting the Christians in the first century to whom the Book of Revelation was originally addressed was Nero Caesar who reigned A.D. 54 to 68. If the Book of Revelation was written in the 90's during the reign of Domitian, John along with other Christians, would have seen Domitian (AD 81–96) as Nero *redivivus*, who according to the myth would come back from the dead to reclaim his throne. This would be, according to Mitchell Reddish, "a powerful means of speaking of evil incarnated in the office of the emperor."[31] In the eyes of the early Christian Nero was a monster who had his wife killed, engaged in many sexual perversions, persecuted and tortured Christians and put them to death in his circus games. Many believe that Nero's official name and title have the numerical value for the infamous number six hundred and sixty-six in Revelation 13:18. LaHaye states that the plain sense of the text "comprises the numbers: six, six, six".[32] But Gary DeMar, a conservative scholar, who has written widely on prophecy, however, believes the three Greek letters should be rendered instead as 600, 60, and 6.[33] DeMar believes that the first readers of Revelation would have calculated the Beast's number as six hundred and sixty-six and with relative ease would have surmised that it was Nero.[34] A textual variant gives the number as 616 Some scholars have speculated that the scribe who changed "666" to "616" was doing so because of a variant spelling of Nero's name.[35] They would not have been looking to some distant future person. That

28. Aune, *Word Bible Commentary*, 732–34.
29. Ibid.,756; Beasley-Murray, *The Book of Revelation*, 206.
30. Maahs, *Of Angels, Beasts and Plagues*, 201.
31. Reddish, *Revelation*, 251.
32. LaHaye, *Revelation Unveiled*, 226–27.
33. DeMar, *End Times Fiction*, 143.
34. Ibid., 143.
35. Reddish, *Revelation*, 261–62.

monstrous beast was either a present reality to them then or would soon arise to cause suffering and persecution.

## THE MARK OF THE BEAST

Drawing on Revelation 13:16–18, LaHaye and Jenkins have stressed the importance of the Mark of the Beast. In the novel, *The Mark*, every man, woman and child has to receive the mark either on their foreheads or right hand. The mark was either the name of Nicolae or the prescribed number—666. "Those who neglect to get the mark when it is made available will not be allowed to buy or sell until such time as they receive it. Those who overtly refuse shall be put to death . . ."[36] The authors focus an entire book in the *Left Behind* series on Nicolae Carpathia's, the Antichrist, requirement that every one had to bear the Beast's mark of 666 or be beheaded. This book notes that everyone, because of the Antichrist's requirement that people bear the mark, is forced into making a decision of whether he or she will accept this mark and worship Nicolae or refuse and be killed by the guillotine. No one can remain neutral. All of those who received the mark demonstrated that they have rejected Christ and will receive eternal punishment in the lake of fire.

What is the mark like? *The New English Bible* translates verse 17 in chapter 13 of Revelation as "to be branded with a mark." Like the mark from a cattle branding iron or a tattoo, a mark could easily have been affixed to a person's hand or forehead. This was routinely done to a slave in ancient times. It would have been clearly visible to the eye and would not require any special "high-tech" way of seeing it. Declaring that only now in history can this mark really be made because of new technology, LaHaye writes that the mark is really a "miniature biochip" that is inserted under the skin.[37] This assertion is a way of declaring that only now with our new technologies is the time right for the Antichrist to appear. Again LaHaye moves away from his own literal interpretation because the Greek preposition in Revelation 13:16 is closely translated "upon" or "on" not "in". The visible mark could easily have been made centuries ago.

It is amazing the many ways of speculation that have surrounded the number 666. People have sometimes demanded new telephone numbers, social security cards or license plates because they contained the numbers

---

36. LaHaye and Jenkins, *The Mark*, 85.
37. Ibid.

666. They were fearful of being somehow linked to the Antichrist or the powers of evil by that number. As we will examine later in our study of Revelation, much of this book's images are symbolic and are not to be taken literally. In Jewish thought the complete number is 7. Six falls short of that and will always be incomplete. The symbolism is that the powers of the evil beast will fail and not achieve its design to overcome Christ's Kingdom. The mark of the Beast, I believe, is a sign of anyone who has denied Christ and chooses to align him or herself with the evil forces that oppose his way. LaHaye has taken a biblical symbol and built a large number of books around interpreting it literally.

## THE FALSE PROPHET

In the *Left Behind* novels Carpathia's right hand man is Leon Fortunate, who is called "The False Prophet". Everything he says and does is to support and further the cause of Carpathia whom he proclaims as the risen god. He eventually rises to the position as the "Most High Reverend Father of Carpathianism" to force people to receive that mark of the Beast and worship the Antichrist. LaHaye bases this figure on Revelation 13:11–18. He clearly distinguished the two beasts. The first one described in Revelation 13:1–10 is "the governmental leader" called the Antichrist who will proclaim himself as god and the second one, described in Revelation 13:11–18, will be the religious leader who will erect an image of the Antichrist and rouse the people to worship the Antichrist.[38]

## THE JEWISH TEMPLE

The first Jewish Temple was built by Solomon and was destroyed by the Babylonians in 586 B.C. The second temple was begun in 535 and finished in 516 B.C. and then renovated by Herod the Great in 19 B.C. The Romans destroyed it in A.D. 70. Prophecy expoundants believed that a third temple would be rebuilt someday. LaHaye places that event during the "Great Tribulation". Carpathia, in the *Left Behind* series, persuades the Muslims to dismantle and move the Dome of the Rock to the new capital in Babylon where a new mosque will be established as a Holy place for Muslims. In the other part of the covenant with Israel, this would free the Temple Mount so the Jews could rebuild the Temple.[39] Later Carpathia,

---

38. LaHaye, *Revelation Unveiled*, 222.
39. LaHaye and Jenkins, *Tribulation Force*, 295.

the Antichrist, will desecrate the temple by offering a hog as a sacrifice on the altar and calling for people to worship him as god. This desecration will usher in the Great Tribulation and God's judgments will be poured out upon the earth.[40]

LaHaye believes that it was impossible to discuss the rebuilding of the Jewish temple fifty years ago. He asserts that we are "on the verge of seeing a third temple built in fulfillment of prophecy" and this is "powerful evidence" that we have more reasons to believe Christ could return in our lifetime than any generation before us.[41]

## NEW BABYLON

Nicolae Carpathia makes a decision to move the U.N. and his world headquarters in *Left Behind*, from New York City to Babylon. "He wants to move it to Babylon." "You're not serious." "He is." "I hear they've been renovating that city for years. Millions of dollars invested in making it, what, New Babylon?"[42] The city of Babylon, on the Euphrates River, is located fifty miles south of Baghdad in modern Iraq. Readers do not understand that LaHaye believes that "the city of Babylon must be restored before the Second Coming."[43] He bases this on what he calls unfulfilled prophecies about the destruction of the city that he sees in Isaiah 13 and 14, Jeremiah 50 and 51, and Revelation 17 and 18.

Nevertheless, LaHaye believes that next to Jerusalem, Babylon is the city mentioned most often in the Bible. He finds 280 references to it. According to him, it was the most important pagan city that ever existed and its influence touched many nations and cities for several centuries. He also locates it as the headquarters of Satan who seeks to attract us through the power of government and commerce as well as religion[44] The *Left Behind* series depicts Babylon as the center of the Antichrist who controls the world governmentally, economically, commercially and religiously. When Christ comes in his Glorious Appearing, the city of Babylon is destroyed completely.[45]

40. LaHaye and Jenkins, *Desecration*,104f.
41. LaHaye and Jenkins, *Are We Living in the End Times?*, 129.
42. LeHaye and Jenkins, *Left Behind*, 352.
43. LaHaye and Jenkins, *Are We Living in the End Times?*, 134.
44. Ibid., 132–33.
45. LaHaye and Jenkins, *Glorious Appearing*, 46.

## THE TWO WITNESSES

"No one ever saw them come or go; none knew where they came from ... but if Buck had to guess, he would have said they were the two Old Testament characters themselves."[46] The two witnesses in the *Left Behind* series were supernatural prophets who did astonishing miracles and gave witness to God's grace in Jerusalem during the first 1,260 days of the Tribulation. LaHaye identifies the two witnesses as Moses and Elijah. Their witness serves to bring many Jews to Christ. After they finish their testimony, the Two Witnesses are killed by the Antichrist. But after three and a half days, God brings them back to life and they ascend to heaven.[47]

Again LaHaye takes these images from Revelation 11:13 literally and builds a powerful call to repentance from these two strange figures from ages long past. Agreeing with LaHaye that the Two Witnesses might symbolize Moses and Elijah, would it not be more reasonable to see them as the voices that continue to bear witness to the law and prophetic word of God and those that died as martyrs for Christ doing a time of persecution? Could John be reminding the early Christians during severe persecution, that Christ needed faithful witnesses who would be rewarded by the assurance of eternal life with God? Is there not a continuing need across the ages for Christians to be faithful witnesses who call men and women to respond to God's redeeming grace? May they not be the continuing witness of the Christian's call to fidelity?

## THE 144,000 JEWISH WITNESSES

During the days of the Tribulation, the *Left Behind* series depicts a world wide evangelism effort which is done by the 144,000 witnesses described in Revelation 7:1–4. "I stand before you with the unique privilege," Tsion Ben-Judah, former rabbinical scholar who was converted to Christ, declared, "I believe, of addressing many of the 144,000 witnesses prophesied in the Scriptures. I count myself one of you ... "[48] These witnesses were drawn from all the nations, races, sexes and the wide variety of languages in the earth. These Jewish evangelists, according to LaHaye, will have the seal of God on one's forehead as a sign of belief, but this will be visible only to other believers. This Christians "seal" is in contrast to the "mark

---

46. LaHaye and Jenkins, *Apollyon*, 134.
47. LaHaye and Jenkins, *Tribulation Force*, 309, 341ff.
48. LaHaye and Jenkins, *Apollyon*, 47.

of the beast". Tsion tells Buck that they have the seal that the Book of Revelation describes in chapter seven. "Tsion seemed to stare desperately at Buck. Suddenly he said, 'Yes, Cameron! We have the seal, visible only to other believers.'"[49]

In the *Left Behind* series even in the last days, hours and moments before the Glorious Appearing of Christ, these witnesses lead millions to find faith in Christ. Moving from fiction to today's world, LaHaye believes that what he calls the rapid spread of the gospel around the world today is "one more powerful evidence that we may be the generation that turns the task over to those who will complete it—the 144,000 Spirit-filled witnesses who will preach to the world shortly after Jesus raptures His Church."[50]

Some have tried to limit the redeemed to only the 144,000 persons in heaven. The writer, John, in Revelation is not giving a limited number but instead is describing the totality of all the faithful. The number is symbolic, I believe, to affirm the whole or complete number of Christians throughout time who will be believers. 144,000 are not to be taken literally but depict a limitless group of people. Some scholars believe that the number 144,000 might be symbolic of those who died as martyred saints. They paid the ultimate sacrifice for Christ and the martyrs under the altar in Chapter 6 ask how long before they will be vindicated. They are told they must wait until the number of martyred saints reaches 144,000.[51]

## THE GREAT APOSTASY

One of the themes that is set forth in the *Left Behind* fiction is what LaHaye calls an end time apostasy. According to him, before Christ will return and rapture his Church, there will be a major movement within the Church toward modernism and rejection of what he believes is the essential Christian beliefs. Some of those who fall into this modern apostasy group, according to LaHaye, are organizations like the Federal Council of Churches established in the 1940's, later the National Council of Churches and the World Council of Churches, the teaching of those he calls the apostate professors in many of the seminaries, and liberal ministers and priests, like John Shelby Spong, Episcopal bishop of Newark,

---

49. LaHaye and Jenkins, *Soul Harvest*, 193.
50. LaHaye and Jenkins, *Are We Living in the End Times?*, 313.
51. Caird, *The Revelation of St. John the Divine*, 94ff.

New Jersey, who championed doctrines that he believed are in keeping with "the religious humanist variety of Unitarianism."[52]

In the *Left Behind* series, a character named Peter Matthews, a contemptuous mimicry of contemporary world religious leaders, becomes the new "pope" with the title Pontifex Maximus Peter. He ushers in what is called "a new era of tolerance and unity" among major religions. The new religious headquarter is set up in Enigma Babylon. He declares that the biggest enemy of the quest for peaceful unity is the intolerance and disunity of the "heretical" beliefs of the Jewish and Christian believers who think their final authority is found in the Old and New Testament Bible, and especially those who believe that Jesus is the only means of salvation. All divisions in denominations and the variety of world religions are removed and "an apostate one-world religion" is established under the Antichrist, Nicolae Carpathia.[53]

Gary DeMar questions LaHaye's insistence that apostasy is an end time event that will occur in the "last days". He reminds his readers that apostasy has been an ongoing struggle in the church's history from the very beginning. For the first-century Christians, there was always the temptation to return to Judaism or to some pagan god they may have worshipped. Apostasy was a real battle for the first believers.[54] Paul challenged the believers not to be ashamed of the gospel (Rom. 1:16) and John warned the first century Christians, "Dear Children, This is the last hour; and as you have heard that the Antichrist is coming, even now many Antichrist have come. This is how we know it is the last hour" (1 John 1:18, New International Version). Apostasy was clearly something that had already happened in the young church and was to them a sign that they were in the last days. They expected Jesus to return soon, in their lifetime likely. But his Second Coming has been delayed, and the church still looks for the end of history as we know it.

---

52. LaHaye and Jenkins, *Are We Living in the End Times?*, 68. See also LaHaye's earlier book, written in 1972, *The Beginning of the End*, 96–103, in which he makes similar accusations.

53. LaHaye and Jenkins, *Tribulation Force*, 401.

54. DeMar, *End Times Fiction*, 174ff.

## ARMAGEDDON

An entire novel is devoted by LaHaye and Jenkins to the Battle of Armageddon, and the conflict is carried over into the twelfth book, *Glorious Appearing*. The conflict is drawn from Revelation 16:12–16. The word Armageddon occurs only in Revelation 16:16. It is the large Valley or Plain of Jezreel in northern Israel where a small hill with a big flat top called Megiddo lies above it. It was the place where several battles took place that are recorded in the Old Testament (Josh. 12:12, Judg. 5:19; 2 Kgs. 23:29). It is the place that LaHaye and other premillennialists believe will be the final conflict Christ will have with the forces of evil and the Antichrist before he begins the thousand-year reign of peace. The Valley of Jehoshaphat, Edom and the city of Jerusalem are also seen as a part of this final battle. LaHaye follows the premillennial view that also envisions the Euphrates River drying up before the final battle that allows the kings from the east to join forces in this conflict.

The *Left Behind* fictional account of Armageddon combines ancient images of thousands of soldiers on horseback with rifles along with all kinds of modern military forces like Hummers, SUV's, armored carriers, grenade and missile launchers, planes, choppers and elaborate technological equipment as a part of Carpathia, the Antichrist's army. The combination of the ancient images drawn from the Scriptures and the new military weapons of today seems an unlikely union for a biblical literalist like LaHaye. Because of the location of the Armageddon in the Middle East, end times prophets have an inclination to see any kind of conflict, especially in Israel or Iraq, as a positive sign that the catastrophic battle on the plains of Megiddo is about to begin. Mitchell G. Reddish, a New Testament scholar who has a specialty in apocalyptic literature, reminds us that the images in Revelation are not to be taken literally and this includes the references to Armageddon. "Armageddon symbolizes," he observes, "the final desperate struggle of evil against the overwhelming power and goodness of God."[55]

## VARIOUS VISIONS

The next chapter will examine the meaning and nature of apocalyptic literature in more detail, but it might be helpful to the reader to sense the basic meaning of some of the many visions or signs John writes about in

---

55. Reddish, *Revelation*, 319.

the Book of Revelation. John's dramatic book utilizes colors, geography, numbers, animals and symbols to communicate its message about the power and presence of Christ during a time of persecution and suffering. LaHaye and Jenkins' end times fiction paints these figures in vivid, literal ways. It might be useful to grasp the purpose most scholars believe John intended for them when he wrote the Apocalypse.

## THE FOUR HORSEMEN

### (Revelation 6:1–8)

Each of these horses symbolized to John four images of the power and might of the Roman Empire's impact on humanity. A painting by Albrecht Durer of "The Four Horsemen of the Apocalypse" presents a dramatic image of a literal interpretation of these figures in Revelation.

*The White Horse*—The conquering powers of Rome.
*The Red Horse*—War
*The Black Horse*—Famine
*The Pale Green Horse*—Death

## THE TRUMPETS

### (Revelation 8:5–11:18)

The trumpet represents God's powerful judgment, but it also delineates God's great mercy. The plagues are sent by God, hopefully, to lead persons to repentance, but at the end, people curse God rather than offering praise. The first five of the seven plagues destroy the earth's greenery, the sea, the rivers, and the heavenly bodies. LaHaye and Jenkins have given almost science fiction images to the monstrous locusts that attack and torture sinful persons and to the hybrid, prodigious horses with heads like lions and tails like serpents and mouths that spew fire. Their destruction in the novels is frightful and shocking. The horses are allowed to kill only a third of humanity. But those who survive still do not repent.

## THE BOWLS

LaHaye draws on Revelation 15:5–16:21 for the vision of the last seven judgments. He sees the emptying of these bowls as the "targets of God's anger".[56] The first bowl of judgment and wrath is poured out on those who had the mark of the beast and they get plagues and malignant sores. The second bowl is poured into the sea and turns it to blood. The third one also turns the rivers and streams into blood. The fourth bowl increases the intensity of the sun and the heat scorches persons with fire. The fifth bowl is emptied on the throne of the beast, which the fiction writers identify as New Babylon, and the city is plunged into darkness so severe that people gnaw their own tongues. The sixth bowl is poured out on the Euphrates River and causes it to dry up and provide a way for the kings in the east to bring their armies to Israel for the final battle of Armageddon. The seventh and final bowl is poured out on the air and causes severe lightning, thunder and other empyreal disturbances before the world's greatest earthquake occurs.[57]

As we have examined some aspects of the *Left Behind* theology in this Chapter, I have tried to indicate that LaHaye's and Jenkins' interpretation focuses on a proof-texting and literal use of Scripture, and it is often found defective. There are other more adequate theological and hermeneutical approaches to the Bible's end times themes. The reader is not restricted or limited by their approach. The next chapter will apprise the reader of other possible interpretations of eschatology and apocalyptic literature.

---

56. LaHaye and Jenkins, *Glorious Appearing*, 104.
57. Ibid., 104–6.

4

## Alternative Understandings

APOCALYPTIC LITERATURE LIKE THE Book of Revelation and Daniel are very difficult for most people to understand. Many find the Book of Revelation with its unusual images and weird creatures not only strange but also mystifying and unintelligible. For that reason Revelation, Daniel and other apocalyptic portions of the Bible are often neglected, ignored and dismissed by many laypersons. Most ministers seldom preach on these obscure writings. For some preachers, however, these books have become the "happy hunting grounds" for wild speculations, eccentric interpretations and the chief source for "doomsday" and end times prophecy. The end times fiction by Tim LaHaye and Jerry Jenkins would certainly fall into this last category. The *Left Behind* novels have not only heralded themselves as *the* authentic and conclusive truth about what will happen in the last days but also as *the* valid interpreter of the Book of Revelation and other apocalyptic literature. On *60 Minutes*, Tim LaHaye was bold to declare, "The books may be fiction but they are based on hard facts."[1] Many readers, unfamiliar with other possible biblical interpretations, assume that these stories of fiction are reliable and acceptable interpretations of the Bible.

As surprising or astounding as it may be to some readers of the *Left Behind* series, I want to alert them to the fact that many of the finest biblical scholars today and throughout the history of the church have proposed entirely different interpretations of books like Revelation, Daniel and other apocalyptic literature than LaHaye and Jenkins have projected in their fictional writings. In this chapter I want to apprise the reader of some of the major interpretations which have been given to the Book of Revelation and the doctrine of the Last Things.

---

1. 60 Minutes, 2/8/04.

## APOCALYPTIC LITERATURE

The first word in the Greek text of the Book of Revelation is the word from which we get the English word Apocalypse. Our English word Revelation, which means to reveal, uncover or disclose, is the translation of this Greek word. This type of literature probably arose from the Persian, Egyptian and Greek religions that the Jewish people first became acquainted with during their exile in Babylon. During the interbiblical period, the time between the writings of the Old Testament books and the New Testament books, this was a very common well-known type of literature.

Some apocalyptic literature may have had an influence on certain of our New Testament writings and was very familiar to many persons in the ancient world, and some even considered it to be sacred literature. Two centuries before the beginning of Christianity *The Book of Enoch* (c.164 B.C.) was written and it is quoted in Jude 14–15. Enoch, the man who "walked with God" (Genesis 5:22), is depicted in this book as having visions of the fall of angels. He seeks to restore the angels to God's favor but cannot and then foresees the "Son of Man" coming as judge and the Anointed One. Another such book was *The Assumption of Moses* (6–30 A.D.), which is quoted in Jude 9. Other Jewish apocalyptic writings include *Jubilees* (150 B.C.), *2 Esdras, 2 Baruch* or *Apocalypse of Baruch* (70 A.D.), *2 Enoch* (1st century A.D.), and the *Apocalypse of Abraham* (1st to 2nd century), and other Christian apocalypses like *The Apocalypse of Peter* (2nd century A.D.) and *The Book of Elchasai* (2nd century). Mitchell G. Reddish, who has done extensive research in the area of apocalyptic literature, lists in his commentary thirteen examples of Jewish apocalypse and twenty-three examples of Christian apocalypses dating from the third century B.C. to the 11th century A.D.[2] Eugene Boring gives twenty-three representatives of Jewish apocalyptic literature known in the ancient world.[3] These types of Jewish apocalypses were very popular and circulated widely in the first century and were well known to the readers of the Book of Revelation. They probably experienced the many other Christian representations of this type of literature that began to be written around the same time as the Book of Revelation. Other apocalyptic literature in the Bible would include Daniel 2:7–12; Ezekiel 1 and other sections as well; Isaiah 24–27; Zechariah 12–14; much of Joel, especially 2:1–32; 1 Thessalonians 4:13–18; 2 Thessalonians

---

2. Reddish, *Revelation*, 6. See also Redditt, "Apocalyptic Literature," 36–38.
3. Boring, *Revelation*, 38–39.

2:1–12; Jude and 2 Peter 2:1–3:18. The references by Jesus in three of the Gospels are also seen as apocalyptic: Matthew 24, Mark 13, Luke 7:22–37, and 21:5–36. Although the Book of Revelation might seem puzzling and abstruse to readers today, the first century recipients would not have found this to be the case for them.

## CHARACTERISTICS OF APOCALYPTIC LITERATURE

It is always risky to try to summarize the major tenets of apocalyptic literature because any simplification might overlook some of the differences, especially as found in the Book of Revelation. Nevertheless, there are certain features that are common to most apocalyptic writings. The following summary is given to help the reader understand the nature of the Bible's apocalyptic literature in the context of other literature of this genre of the time.

## CRISIS OR PERSECUTION

Most apocalypses were written during a period of crisis, suffering, or persecution, whether political, social or theological. This is certainly true of the Book of Revelation. The powers of the government or forces of evil seem to be dominant and the Jews or Christians struggled to ascertain where God was during this critical time.

The Book of Revelation was written to Christians who were being persecuted for their beliefs and especially their rejection of the worship of the emperor. Since this was a national religion, they were considered as "atheists" because of their refusal to comply with the totalitarian demands. References have been found to Nero's persecution of the Christians in A.D. 64 and to Domitian's persecution as well. It was during the reign of Domitian (A.D. 81–96) that the Book of Revelation was likely written. There are some scholars on the other hand who believe that it was unlikely that there was any organized persecution of Christians by the Romans in Asia Minor during the last decade of the first century. "Two decades later, however," Richard Vinson notes "the Roman governor of the neighboring province would execute Christians who failed to worship the emperor's cult image and begin two centuries of off-again, on-again imperial persecution of Christianity."[4] Either the Christians of that day were

---

4. Richard Vinson, "The Social World of the Book of Revelation," *Review and Expositor* ( 98, Winter 2001), 29.

facing eminent persecution, or they were too comfortable with practices that John considered too worldly, or he was warning them of persecution that was to happen soon, and he was exhorting them to remain faithful even if it meant that they would have to suffer for their Christian faith. In Chapter 13 of Revelation the Roman Empire is depicted as a beast that demands worship and who kills all who refuse to comply. John, the writer of Revelation, indicates that he was exiled to Patmos for his preaching against these practices (1:9) and he mentions one person, Antipas (2:13), who had been martyred in Pergamum. In many places throughout the Book of Revelation Christians are warned of this time of testing, and John called them to be faithful to Christ and not give in to the demands of the "beast".

## TWO AGES

In most apocalyptic writings the present age was seen as controlled by the powers of evil and the righteous ones cannot prevail against its monstrous authority. Consequently, they often suffer and are persecuted and put to death. Difficulties, trials and sufferings will continue until the last days when God will usher in a new age that will be pain free, beautiful and with God in complete control. John clearly follows this apocalyptic distinction of the present evil age of suffering and persecution and the assurance of the new age that will be ushered in by Christ. The age under the control of the "beast" and the Antichrist will be overcome ultimately by God's own redeeming action.

## COSMIC DUALISM

In apocalyptic thinking the two stages are a reminder that a powerful dualism exist in the world between the forces of good and the rulers of evil. This dualism depicted the classical primeval conflicts of order and chaos, the fall of humanity, the rebellion of angels, wars in heaven and the continuing struggle between God and Satan, good and evil and in some cases, like in Revelation, Christ and the Antichrist, God and Satan. Angels and demons are also seen as a part of this dualism. They are messengers for good or evil. Revelation abounds with both. The present age is seen as under the control of the powers of evil—Satan. The age to come will restore God's ultimate control once more. During the present conflict, Satan and the demonic powers of evil are engaged in a struggle with God and the angels for control over humanity and the present world. Humanity battles not just selfishness but "principalities and powers" (Eph 6:10–12) with supernatural resources. Humanity cannot overcome these powers by sheer personal effort because they are too perverse. God's intervention is essential for a certain victory. Some apocalyptic writings describe Satan and God as equal contenders in the struggle for this world, but Revelation never depicts Satan with the same power as God.

John clearly notes an apocalyptic dualism, but God's sovereignty is affirmed and a strong monotheism underlies his writing. The powers of evil—the "beast"—are evident but God is never seen as remote or uncaring about the world or Christians. Every human system, whether it is political, religious or some other structure, always stands under the judgment of the one true God. God is always in control and the outcome of the struggle between the two worlds set against each other is foreordained. This world may not be salvaged but there will be a new world, a new heaven that God will establish.

## PESSIMISM

Apocalyptitic writings usually hold a pessimistic view of the world. This is natural since they see the present age under the control of Satan and evil rulers. They see no real hope for the present world situation to change and see the powers of evil prevailing until the new age comes. Apocalyptic readers are encouraged not to be enslaved by the powers of evil and darkness, but to remain faithful to God during the difficult days. Ultimately, they are assured, God will prevail and bring lasting justice and peace. Revelation is not a book of despair and hopelessness but rings with the assurance of God's ultimate victory over the powers of evil with a new heaven and a new earth. John's assurance that God is in control and sovereign offers hope and encouragement to its readers.

## A CALL FOR FIDELITY

In the present evil age, especially as seen in Revelation, the reader is urged to be faithful. The reader is encouraged to hold on; God will bring victory to those who remain faithful. During a time of suffering, persecution and trial, it is easy to because discouraged and to fall away (apostatize) from one's faith in God. Apocalyptic literature is like a "watchman" urging the readers to stand firm and not give in to the evil forces because in the final struggles, they are assured God will prevail. Apocalyptic literature may be pessimistic about the present age and see an ongoing struggle between good and evil, but ultimately, the writers are optimistic because they believe that God will prevail and save his people and bring in a glorious new age.

The watchword of Revelation seems to be found in 2:10 "Be faithful even to the point of death, and I will give you the crown of life." The message to the seven churches and throughout the Book of Revelation is a challenge to fidelity. God, they are assured, has not abandoned them; therefore they are urged to trust God and not to compromise their beliefs. The Church is seen as being engaged in a life-and-death struggle with the powers of the world and Satan. The Christians were summoned not to compromise with the Roman authorities' demand to accept the religious images of the state but to maintain their loyalty to Christ. In his book, *Engaging the Powers*, Walter Wink states that John in the Book of Revelation is "referring explicitly to the Domination System currently embodied in the Roman Empire. 'The kingdom of the world (*kosomos*)' (11:15) for him is not a geographical or planetary term. It refers to the alienated and alienating reality that seduces humanity into idolatry: the worship of political power as divine." He observes that the Roman Empire demanded the worship of the spirituality of the empire. "The Roman Empire had made itself the highest value and the ultimate concern, arrogating to itself the place of God."[5] John warned Christians of this idolatry and challenged them to be faithful to Christ, even if it meant the ultimate sacrifice— one's death.

## THE PROVIDENCE OF GOD

It is interesting that most apocalyptic writings issued in a call to faithfulness, yet many readers struggled with the faithfulness of God during their time of suffering and persecution. They must have asked questions like the following: "Where is God during this difficult time?" "Why does God not help his people and defend them against the forces of evil?" "When persons saw their loved one's die, their concern was not with some distant or remote historical event, what they demanded to know was," 'where is God in this moment that I need divine assistance?'" "God had promised to bless his people and be with them. Where is God now?"

No simple, easy answer to these questions is given in apocalyptic writings. But a big, bold picture of God is presented as the One who is

---

5. Wink, *Engaging the Powers*, 300.

in control of history and who will determine its final picture. God not Satan, good not evil will have the final word. God is the Almighty who is Creator and sovereign and remains faithful to those who are faithful to God. The providence and sovereignty of God are affirmed. In Revelation John reminds his readers that God has declared, "'I am the Alpha and the Omega,' say the Lord God, 'who is and who was, and who is to come, the almighty'" (Rev 1:8). Revelation reminds its readers that God does not act in a malevolent manner but ministers through the sacrificial activity of the Lamb of God (Rev 5:6–14).

Jesus Christ is called the Lamb twenty-nine times in Revelation. This image reminds us that God's use of power is not coercive or vindictive but loving, sacrificial, suffering and redeeming. Apocalyptic writers, and especially Revelation, assure their readers that God is still in control no matter how powerful or perverse evil powers may appear. God has the final word. It is a word of hope and assurance. It is also a reminder that God is neither remote, transcendent or uncaring but is there with his people and will eventually lead them into a new age. So rather than being vague or obscure, apocalyptic writers sought to give a practical word to encourage their readers and give hope to fainting spirits. This may indeed have been their primary aim.

## PSEUDONYMOUS AUTHORSHIP

The writers of most apocalyptic literature usually wrote under the name of some great leader from the past like Abraham, Moses, Enoch, Ezra or the like. Rather than using his or her own name, this method was done in hopes of getting a wider reading or audience. These "pseudonymous" names may also have been used to conceal the identify of the real writer to protect him or her from the political or religious leaders who might want to punish someone who condemned their leadership or reign. Revelation, however, does not follow this usual pattern. The author clearly reveals his name and makes no attempt to disguise it. His name seems to have been well known and respected by the Christians in Asia to whom he was writing. Four times in Revelation the writer refers to himself as John (Rev 1:1, 4, 9; 22:8). This John seems to have been well known by his readers but his identity has been the subject of much scholarly debate. Some have seen the writer as the Apostle John while others in the early church thought it was some other John who may have been a disciple of the apostle; others have projected still another John called "John the Presbyter" or "John the Elder" or maybe some "unknown" Christian prophet named John.

Most contemporary biblical scholars do not believe that the disciple John could be the author because of internal evidence like 21:14 that refers to the twelve apostles whose names were written on the foundation of the New Jerusalem. He would hardly have made this kind of reference to himself. He also does not give any indication of knowing Jesus personally. Revelation, according to most scholars, was probably written in A.D. 95 which would make the disciple from Zebedee to be in his nineties. The most reliable scholarship views the writer of Revelation as someone named John who was familiar to his readers, likely lived somewhere in Asia Minor, and probably wrote his book in the latter part of the first century. He cannot be identified accurately today. This in no way, however, detracts from the significance of the book but may simply add to its mystery. The authors of many books in the Bible are unknown, but we still accept them as a part of Holy Scripture.

## SYMBOLISM AND VISIONS

One of the most apparent and well-known features of apocalyptic writing is its vivid and detailed use of symbols, visions and other images. The writers often describe their strange vision of animals, birds or other creatures in fantastic details. Look at Ezekiel's picture of the four living creatures and wheels (Ezek. 1:4–24; 10) and the four living creatures and beasts in Revelation (Rev 4:6–11; 13:1–18). Much use is made of numbers like two, three, four, five, six, seven, ten, ten thousand times ten thousand and 666 and others. Colors, geography, animals and other symbols are employed to communicate the writer's message. "The language of apocalyptic is *symbolic*, not pure code," Maahs reminds us. It communicates through pictures because it is "the language of the artist and poet."[6]

At times these images seem to cause us to wonder what the meaning or message may have been. To the ancient reader, these symbols would have been recognizable, even if they were obscure to pagan political leaders. They served as a vehicle to communicate to the readers of the past words of hope, inspiration and encouragement. The message transmitted through them was not meant to be grasped in some literalistic manner but to "trigger" the imagination of the reader to envision the awesome

---

6. Maahs, *Of Angels, Beasts and Plagues*, 16.

*Alternative Understandings* 57

mystery and power of good and evil, Satan and God, struggle and triumph, and most of all the ultimate Almighty reign of God, who continues to direct and guide history.

The Book of Revelation seems to explode with symbolisms of every description. The reader's imagination is stimulated by images of thrones and crowns, feast and famine, horses and warriors, war and peace, dragon and lamb, Christ and Antichrist, the beast and the Son of Man, Babylon and new Jerusalem, the sea and the land, Satan and God the ox and the lion, eagles and locusts, hail and fire, and countless others. John paints powerful images with a brush of many colors: a white horse, white robes, a white throne, a white stone, a black horse, a green horse, a red horse, a red dragon, a scarlet beast, golden crowns, golden streets, golden harps, a golden girdle, a woman dressed in purple, and others. Places and locations call out to the reader: the sea, rivers, mountains, plains, the temple, the abyss, the lake of fire, New Jerusalem, Babylon, the throne of God, Ephesus, Philadelphia, Laodicea and others. Scripture allusions from the Old Testament abound. Some scholars have counted over four hundred.[7]

The use of numbers in Revelation stagers the imagination: Two for witnessing, seven for the divine number or perfection, six for sin or imperfection, ten for completeness or wholeness, twelve for the church, 144,000 for all true believers, ten-thousand times ten thousand for innumerable, 666 for the beast or the Antichrist, etc. Dramatic images abound: seven-branched lamp stand, seven burning torches, the lamb with seven horns, the four horseman, martyrs under the altar in heaven; hail, fire and blood; bowls of wrath; locusts with human faces, lions' teeth and scorpion tails; a woman clothed in the sun, a beast rising from the sea, bowls of plagues, a beast with seven heads and ten horns, the coming of the new Jerusalem, the illumination of heaven, the river of life and many more.

John used these symbols to awaken the imagination of his readers and to view the powerful struggle between good and evil, God and Satan. These images are not to be taken literally or allegorized because that often would be a denial of their real meaning and message for the age in which they were written and for our age today and for others in the future who read this message of encouragement and hope. Like a chip that needs deciphering, these symbols demand from the reader a careful rendering to grasp the writer's intention. The Book of Revelation is written more from

7. Ford, *Revelation*, 27. See Charles, *A Critical and Exegetical Commentary on the Revelation of St. John*, lxv–lxxxiii.

the pen of a poet, an artist or a musician than from the carefully measured plans or designs of an engineer. The pictures in Revelation point beyond themselves to a deeper meaning. The symbols conceal as well as reveal to protect the Christians from the Roman Empire. In the sense of Paul Tillich's distinction between "sign and symbol",[8] John's symbolism in Revelation points beyond itself to the reality behind them. To try to reduce them to a wooden literalism that can be proven by scientific means or deciphered like some Morse code is to abuse John's original intention to enable believers to live in their world.

## ESCHATOLOGY

Apocalyptic writings are concerned with what is called the "last things" like death, the end of the present age or the consummation of history and the projection of the age to come. Since God is seen as in control of history and is sovereign and almighty, God will determine the outcome and not the powers of evil humanity or demonic forces. Their time is limited and God's time is at hand. The eschatology in these writings affirms that the struggles, persecutions and suffering of the righteous are near an end.

John's basic purpose was to encourage the believers to be faithful and to be assured that God was still in charge of all of history. John wrote Revelation to help his readers face the world in which they lived and not to offer them some timetable about what might happen two hundred, or a thousand or two thousand years later. That would not have been helpful to them at all in facing their present crisis. John was a "prophet" a "forth teller"—one who preached to his listeners the good news about God in their present situation in the first century. The end times events projected in Revelation are seen as occurring in the readers' own lifetimes. Any message to the present generation from Revelation must be based on the reality of the significance the first century Christians found in that word. As the early church found comfort, encouragement and hope in John's *Apocalypse*, so we, too, can hear God's Word spoken to us today through it to guide us in knowing how to live as Christians in our own culture.

---

8. Tillich, *Dynamics of Faith*, 41–54.

*Alternative Understandings* 59

## VARIOUS INTERPRETATIONS OF THE APOCALYPSE

Throughout Christian history the Book of Revelation has been interpretated in many ways. Maybe there have not been as many interpretations of the book as Baskin Robbins has ice cream flavors, or as many viewpoints as Revelation has monsters and strange images, nevertheless, it has been the source of many flavorful, strange and monstrous explanations. R.H. Charles in his critical commentary on Revelation listed nine methods of interpretations.[9] Today others could be added to that list. There are four classical or standard approaches to interpretating Revelation,[10] but I will discuss one earlier method and two more contemporary renderings. Too many readers of the *Left Behind* fiction assume wrongly that LaHaye and Jenkins' literal interpretation of Revelation is *the* only way Revelation can be understood. Most contemporary scholarship takes a completely different perspective.

## THE SPIRITUAL OR ALLEGORICAL UNDERSTANDING

This view in a "nutshell" sees the teachings of Revelation as "timeless truths" that are addressed to no particular historical situation but contain universal and spiritual symbols to communicate eternal truths. This interpretation assumes that since the meaning of the text is not obvious, the hidden meaning can be discerned by using allegory. An allegory depicts people, images, visions and happenings in Revelation with another meaning to explain their significance. This view either ignores the historical setting of the first century readers or is unaware of the crisis setting that gave occasion for the writing of the book in the first place. Although Origen (died 250 A.D.) wrote no commentary on Revelation, he allegorized the book depicting the beast with seven heads in Revelation 13:1–10 as "the seven deadly sins," and identified "the scroll with the seven seals" (Rev 4:1–8:4) with Scriptures. This was a peculiar method in the Alexandrian school of the third century.

Although this method of interpretation for Revelation is suspect today, it seems to me that this approach may still be alive in the way many end times preachers take the figures of the beast, the Antichrist, the number 666, and others and put a modern face on those ancient images

---

9. Charles, *The Revelation of St. John*, clxxxiii–clxxxvii.

10. To examine the classical methods in greater length see Maahs, *Of Angels, Beasts and Plagues*, 19–27 and Boring, *Revelation*, 47–51. See also Keener, *Revelation*, 27–30.

from Revelation. To spiritualize the biblical text to such a degree that one ignores the original setting and purpose for it being written in the first place is a major conflict. This is what LaHaye and Jenkins have done in their *Left Behind* fiction. It is appropriate and essential that Revelation continue to address the contemporary church with its message of hope and encouragement in times of difficulties and crisis. But its message for the first century has to be maintained and not discarded.

## THE PAST TENSE VIEW

This perspective has usually been designated as "The Contemporary-historical" approach. The exponents of the contemporary-historical or the "past tense" view of Revelation believed that the entire apocalyptic message was realized in the days of the Roman Empire of the first century. This view is called the "preterite" method from the Latin, *praetor*, meaning past or beyond. The word contemporary is a reference to John's time in the first century, not our present contemporary setting. These interpreters saw no future dimensions in the *Book of Revelation*. Its message was for its day only. All of the symbolic images in Revelation, according to this interpretation, are John's picture of what was happening in his lifetime. The figures of the two beasts and the dragon are references to Rome. Revelation pictures Rome's rise to its mighty power but relates also its demise.

The seven churches represent the first century church's struggle with the culture and powers of its own day. The way these churches met this challenge of suffering and persecution, as they were empowered by Christ, provides direction for the church to follow as they seek to be faithful to Christ. The difficult issue for most interpreters of Revelation is what does John mean when he has Jesus saying, "I am coming soon" (Rev 22:19 and the vision in chapter 18–22)? How do these interpreters understand the meaning of "soon" or "the time is near"? According to Kenneth Maahs, those who hold this view believe that "the time period is already *past* for the author (John) and the churches noted . . . He is looking back on events that have already transpired."[11] Until the second coming of Christ was finalized, and it was coming soon, John urged the churches to remain faithful. After all, he had already seen the dawn of the new age.

---

11. Maahs, *Of Angels, Beasts and Plagues*, 21.

## PREDICTING FOR THE REMOTE FUTURE

This perspective has often been called the historical approach or the continuous-historical or the world-historical view. This interpretation of Revelation sees the book as prophecy, especially chapters 4–17, that was predicting the history of the Christian Church from its beginning down to the end of time. This prediction offered a complete history of the Christian Church that brought it forward to the time in which the one doing the interpreting lived. They sought to give the successive stages of history to its final fulfillment. Prophecy was seen basically as predictions that affirmed the sovereignty of God in every age. Each age of the Church has seen Revelation as relevant to its own time. What this means is that every interpreter has understood John's predictions in Revelation as related to the age in which the one doing the interpreting lived.

Advocates of this view like to point to some particular person or event in the history of the western civilization as the fulfillment of the various signs in Revelation. It is most interesting that they selected *only* western civilization. They would often point to some evil persons in history and show, according to some special numbering code, how this person was identified by 666. After locating the evil person, they would then show how the other signs in Revelation related to him and were consummated then. They often developed elaborate calendars and times to predict the end.

Martin Luther, for example, was convinced that the Roman Catholic's papacy was the beast in Revelation and bore the number 666. While at the same time, the Roman Catholic Church pointed out that the Latin form of Luther's name was rendered 666. Earlier persons like Victorinus of Pettau (early fourth century) and Joachim of Floris (Twelfth century) each saw the predictions of Revelation as being fulfilled in his own time. LaHaye and Jenkins have certainly adopted the basic philosophy of this school of thought. They see the prediction to occur soon in our own day.

As important as it is for every generation to see how the Apocalypse relates to one's own age, this is a very subjective approach and makes the book meaningless to the readers to whom it was originally written. Through the centuries, those who have embraced this view have fallen into the trap of narrowly defining or limiting the book to predictions about the distant future or remote past and missing its prophetic message of hope and call to faithfulness which continues to be relevant for all time.

This view has seriously missed John's purpose in communicating assurance and guidance to the first century church as well. No serious biblical scholar supports this subjective perspective today.

## THE END TIMES ARE COMING SOON

The perspective that sees the end times coming soon is called the "Futurist" or the end of history view. The prophecy in Revelation is understood basically as predictions about the end of history that have not yet been fulfilled. The Futurist method of interpretation Revelation is usually the one most dispensationalist and premillennialist use. This view has many similarities to the historical approached just mentioned above. Most futurists take the Scriptures literally and see the end times as coming soon, often in their own lifetime as the continuous-historical method did.

Their interpretation of the seven churches mentioned in chapter 2 and 3 of the Book of Revelation is a kind of allegorical approach. These churches are not interpreted as literal churches but are representatives of seven periods of the church history of the apostolic Church of the first century to the apostate church of the last days. The time line of church history and the seven churches are depicted as the Church of Ephesus represents John's, the writer of Revelation, own day in the first century. Smyrna is the period to A.D. 316; Pergamum, the period following A.D. 316; Thyatira represents the Papacy; Sardis is the period of the Protestant Reformation; Philadelphia, the period of the True Church, and Laodicea the period of the final Apostasy.[12] All of this is based on a very inadequate and bogus interpretation from Daniel 9 and a weak theory of "seventy weeks". Most scholars do not believe that Daniel's prophecy or John's writing about the seven churches can possibly be made to fit into such a scheme other than by spiritualizing or allegorizing these passages. This, of course, is not sound biblical exegesis. Like the continuous historical method, this interpretation is highly subjective.

Futurists understand chapters 4–17 in Revelation to predict the final period of the story of humanity. This period will be the seven years of "tribulation" during which believers will be persecuted. Again this view is based on subjection rather than clear biblical teachings. Most of Revelation to the futurists focuses on future events that have not yet happened. Christians will miss the seven years of tribulation, according to

12. Ibid., 25.

these advocates, because they will be raptured (Rev 4:1). After this period of seven years, Christ will return for the persons who have become believers during the period of tribulation and have not worshipped the Beast or the Antichrist. The Futurists' interpretation of the "short time before the end" or "Jesus is coming soon" places this event in the lifetime of those who are making the prediction. The whole futuristic view of the end times robs the original recipients of the significance of the Book of Revelation for them. They could not find strength to be faithful in their day with some notion about God's help in the far distant future.

This amazing view was introduced into the United States by the nineteenth century English preacher named J.N. Darby (mentioned in chapter two), championed by C.I. Scofield, Dallas Theological Seminary, John F. Walvoord, Jerry Falwell and in the nonfiction writings of Tim LaHaye and in the *Left Behind* fiction of the LaHaye and Jerry Jenkins. LaHaye calls himself a Futurist in Theology. He is indeed!

## THE POLITICAL-RELIGIOUS TYPOLOGY VIEW

Advocates of this view draw upon the impact of sociopolitical factors such as the liberation theology of South America, the civil rights struggle, the world AIDS crisis, apartheid in South Africa, the feminist movement in the United States, and the struggle for justice around the world, the ecological crisis, and other significant issues. Their reading of the Book of Revelation is not to distract from its message of encouragement and hope for Christians when they were being persecuted in the first century, but to draw upon the signs, symbols and message of Revelation that they understood and apply the paradigms or typology derived from Revelation to their own struggles today. This reading of the text allows them to find prototypes in Revelation to bring illuminations into their own suffering and injustice in their own situations. "Their interpretations," Adela Yarboro Collins states, "go 'behind' or 'beneath' conscious attitudes to what are considered to be deeper realities."[13]

To oppressed people, rather than being a book that is dull or uninteresting, Revelation speaks to their own world situation in a way it addressed the persecuted Christians in the Roman Empire of the first cen-

---

13. Collins, *Crisis & Catharsis*, 16. See also Collins, *The Combat Myth in the book of Revelation*; Fiorenza, "Toward a Feminist Biblical Hermeneutics," 91–112; and Boesak, *Comfort and Protest*.

tury. They identify with their struggles and sense that Revelation provides them with a way of understanding their own suffering and crisis, but it also helps them name the powers of evil in ways that will motivate them to resist these forces and continue in their struggles for justice, change and liberation. These persons can identify with Revelation's summons to resist the government's oppression. They understand what it is like to be oppressed, demeaned, marginalized and the victim of racial or sexual prejudice. Their interpretation usually motivates its adherents to action.

Allan Boesak's commentary, *Comfort and Protest,* draws on Revelation in his struggle against apartheid in South Africa. Daniel Barrigan offers his understanding of Revelation while in prison for his anti-nuclear-war protests.[14] Brian Blount, Professor of New Testament at Princeton Theological Seminary, reads the *Book of Revelation* through the lens of African American culture in his book, *Can I Get a Witness?*[15] Elisabeth Schussler Fiorenza provides a powerful commentary, *Revelation Vision of a Just World* that is a critical feminist political interpretation of the *Apocalypse* that focuses on its rhetorical persuasive power. Adela Yarboro Collins's *Crisis & Catharsis: The Power of the Apocalypse* provides a post critical analysis of Revelation and seeks to understand the psychological meaning and social themes behind the text as she reflected on the social milieu of the time of persecution in the Roman Empire of the first century. Although a typological, sociological and rhetorical method of analysis for Revelation certainly has its limitations, it does offer a reading of Revelation that may approximate John's intention in writing the book in the first place.

## THE DRAMATIC-LITERARY VIEW

The Dramatic-literary interpretation views Revelation as a "drama" or a "dramatic letter" or some type of literary piece that contains plot, characters and themes. These advocates maintain that the visual elements of the book were to be heard and seen if they were to be understood. The author of Revelation drew upon Greek tragic drama as the literary medium to communicate his message to the believers of the first century. The "epistle" was not really supposed to be read but seen and heard like a Greek drama. This approach believes that the visionary and audio experiences

---

14. Fiorenza, *Revelation*, 11.
15. Blount, *Can I Get a Witness?*

of Revelation necessitated a dramatic presentation for the first century audience to grasp its message for its own day and can best be understood by a contemporary audience as they see it presented in a dramatic production as well.

Scholars who have espoused this view have recognized a dramatic dimension in The *Book of Revelation* that has separated it from the rest of the New Testament writings. John himself has seen visions, heard music and experiences the presence of God in a special way. His record of his experiences is written in a visionary fashion that really calls for the "epistle" to be read aloud to the churches. The writer is both a seer who has had visions and one who has heard important words, but, as Jacques Ellul observes, "he is first of all the one who sees the personages, the scenes, the scenario of events."[16]

The foremost advocate of this interpretation, known to me, is James L. Blevins, who was Professor of New Testament Interpretation at the Southern Baptist Theological Seminary in Louisville, Kentucky for many years. His article on "The Book of Revelation" in the *Mercer Dictionary of the Bible* states clearly that this is his approach.[17] He has also written a book entitled *Revelation As Drama* in which he offers guidelines and a drama script for churches to present *The Book of Revelation* as a drama. He saw the dramatic flavor of the *Book of Revelation*, and viewed it as having been written in seven acts, each with seven scenes. Through the years, Dr. Blevins has had students present Revelation as a drama in the seminary chapel. Blevins has wondered if John might not have been inspired by the seven windows in the theater in Ephesus as a model for his writing. Blevins had hoped that his writing might be presented in this famous theater.[18]

Over fifty years ago, Edward A. McDowell, who also taught New Testament at Southern Baptist Theological Seminary in Louisville, Kentucky and at Southeastern Baptist Theological Seminary in Wake Forest, North Carolina, interpreted Revelation as "the Great Drama of the Sovereignty of God" in two dramatic acts, each with seven scenes.[19] Another person who takes the dramatic approach to understanding

---

16. Ellul, *Apocalypse*, 21.
17. Blevins, "Book of Revelation," 761.
18. Blevins, *Revelation As Drama*.
19. McDowell, *The Meaning and Message of The Book of Revelation*.

Revelation is John Wick Bowman, *The First Christian Drama* (Philadelphia: Westminster Press, 1965). The dramatic quality of Revelation has also inspired many artists with vivid paintings like Albrecht Durer, "The Four Horsemen of the Apocalypse", William Blake's "The Last Judgment", and "Death on a Pale Horse", J.M.W. Turner's "The Angel Standing in the Sun" and many others.

The presentation of the *Book of Revelation* as a drama would be a wonderful way for a congregation to grasp its meanings. Few congregations however would be able to undertake such a task but Blevins' book could offer real help. Another way to present the book to a congregation would be in the form of a dramatic reading. Various persons could be assigned different sections of the book to be read orally to a congregation. John may have expected the book to be read in his day since many likely could not read. I question whether John actually expected his Revelation to be performed as a Greek drama.

## THE APOCALYPTIC APPROACH

The Apocalyptic interpretation seeks to draw the best insights it can from the other methods and seeks to move beyond their limitations. The "past tense view" limits the *Book of Revelation* to the first century and the "futurist" focuses on the end of history. This view acknowledges that many of the symbols definitely do apply to their own day—The beast of Rome, seven literal churches, etc., as the "preterits" state. It also affirms the historical approach that situations that occurred in first century Rome may have had similar happenings at other times in history. They would agree with the "futurists" that the vision John had of the world to come of peace and joy was still to be realized.

This approach consistently takes the images and figures of Revelation symbolically and not literally and interprets the message of the Apocalypse as a theology or philosophy of history. This view consistently takes into account what the text, meant to those to whom it was first written before it tries to find some meaning for us today. The symbols of the first century communicated to the first generation of Christians is a typological way that fit into their sociopolitical culture as they waged their conflict with an evil empire. In a similar way today, contemporary believers gain direction from the way the first century Christians addressed their enemy and endured their own suffering. The Church comes to the realization that no matter what time period the Church is in, the first generation or the twenty-first century, our struggle with the enemy that opposes us is always the same. It is a perennial struggle. We are always called to be faithful whatever our struggle is and to find encouragement in the continuous presence of God. The events described symbolically in Revelation are not restricted to the past nor transferred to some remote future but are representations of how things always transpire when good and evil, Christ and culture, love and force collide. We live with the comforting assurance of Revelation that God will ultimately be triumphant.

This approach also takes seriously the historical-critical interpretation of Scripture and seeks to learn from the best of contemporary scholarship and does not ignore or deny its solid insights. It also draws the best insights that relate to Revelation from other disciplines such as psychology, sociology, drama, art, rhetoric, science or any other medium that might offer helpful insights. It sees the other methods as starting points for conversation, but recognizes that they are not necessarily always safe landing fields. The Apocalyptic approach seems to this writer the more valid approach to understanding the real meaning of Revelation and will be used in the next Chapter to look at the method used in LaHaye and Jenkins' end times fiction. M. Eugene Boring reminds us that practically all critical Bible scholars across all theological perspectives have an agreement on interpreting the Book of Revelation.

> Contrary to popular supposition, there is a broad consensus of agreement among such scholars on the interpretation of Revelation, more than for most New Testament Books. This view assumes that John had a message to the churches to which he was writing which concerned their own situation, that they understood the message and that the modern interpreter cannot accept any interpretation of the book which its first readers would not have understood.[20]

As you can see from these seven interpretations, *The Book of Revelation* has been interpreted in various ways. Any interpreter of the *Apocalypse* needs to be aware of the nature of apocalyptic literature, the significance of pictorial and symbolic images, the imaginative nature of such writing, a knowledge of the sociopolitical climate of the ancient world in which it was written, the needs and concerns of the early Christian believers, and then explore and expound the text with fear and humility, not with

---

20. Boring, *Revelation*, 50–51.

arrogance and finality, as though one could possibly have the only insight into this mysterious and inexhaustible writing. Some interpretations obviously have more credence than others. That is the reason I endorse the Apocalyptic approach as the one on the most solid footing. Thomas Long has encouraged ministers to preach and teach about eschatology in his recent Lyman Beecher Lectures entitled *Preaching from Memory to Hope*.[21] Lay persons are indeed interested in this subject and need intelligent guidance in this area.

---

21. Long, *Preaching from Memory to Hope*, 111ff.

# 5

# Discerning the Truth

THE DOCTRINES OF OUR Christian faith are usually built on a strong biblical and theological structure grounded in a long history of tradition with congregational and church conferences and councils affirming those theological tenets. These doctrines have not come into our faith structure for the first time only recently. But they have a long and cherished history. This is not the case for LaHaye and Jenkins' concept of the Rapture. It is a relative recent visitor to the theological agenda.

## THE SPIRE

William Golden has a novel entitled *The Spire*, with its setting in the Bavarian Alps. The story focuses on an elderly priest, named Jocelin, who has been the Dean of an old dilapidated cathedral for a long time. His dream was to put a 450-foot spire on top of the church building to remind the farmers and herdsmen of God while they worked. But it was a poor congregation, and the church building was also a very poorly constructed. He had been told by architects and engineers not to put a spire on top of the building. They said that it simply could not support that kind of load.

When the priest was eighty years old, the only wealthy member in the congregation died and left all of her resources to the church. At last he saw his opportunity to build his 450-foot spire. And the work soon began. In spite of persons, like the engineers and others who said, "Don't do it," the old priest insisted they begin the construction. In erecting the 450-foot spire, the spiritual life of the church was destroyed. Daily mass could not be held because of all the construction noise and the profanity of the workers on the scaffolds. Most of the workers quit because the construction was too dangerous. The priest had to spend many hours trying to get others to join his work crew until the spire was finished.

After the spire was finally finished, it was not the permanent witness that the priest had hoped it would be. Every time the wind blew, the spire creaked, groaned and moved as though it would topple over. He erected his spire, but he had destroyed his church in the process. The structure of the church building was simply not strong enough to sustain it.[1]

## THE RAPTURE

Tim LaHaye and Jerry Jenkins have constructed a Rapture "spire" are their novels that cannot withstand the biblical and theological winds of criticism that have stormed against it. A careful examination of the Scriptures will show that the whole "rapture theme" on which these fiction stories is based is a fabrication that will bring the entire structure down. Not only are their novels fiction but their biblical foundation for these tales is also fiction. No reliable biblical scholar, except a few isolated fundamentalists, substantiates their claims. Readers of these novels should be aware of this fact. Although LaHaye and Jenkins claim that they have broad support, this is not the case. In actuality, many voices of criticism have been raised to challenge their unsubstantiated claims.

In the first of the series of *Left Behind* novels a reference is made to the pastor's Rapture tape. Chloe asked, "His what?" "Our senior pastor loved to preach about the coming of Christ to rapture his church," Barnes noted, "to take believers, dead and alive, to heaven before a period of tribulation on the earth."[2] This tape was left by their church's pastor to address those who were left behind, and it offered guidance to them on how they might became a Christian. These novels depict the Rapture as the physical transportation of the bodies of the believers to be with Jesus in his Father's house. Their clothes were left but they were snatched away in the midst of whatever they were doing. Rayford's wife and son were taken but he and his daughter, Chloe, were not.[3] The rest of the novels are built around Rayford, Chloe and her future husband, Buck, and the response of others to the message about the Rapture and the reality that they were indeed left behind while others had gone to heaven. Some of those left behind become believers and then they have to battle the Antichrist during the period of seven years of the

1. Golden, *The Spire*.
2. LaHaye and Jenkins, *Left Behind*, 194.
3. This theory is emphasized again it the prequel, *The Rapture* by LaHaye and Jenkins, 171ff.

tribulation. This small band of believers becomes what is called "the tribulation force," a sort of "Christian A-Team" or a "Mission Impossible" unit that works to undermine the efforts of Satan and to reach others for Christ. This Rapture notion makes for interesting fiction but can it be supported with solid biblical evidence?

## RESPONSE TO THE RAPTURE THEORY

To LaHaye, the Rapture and the second coming are viewed as two separate occurrences. Even LaHaye acknowledges that "no one passage of Scripture teaches the two phases of Christ's second coming separated by the Tribulation."[4] He does believe, however, that "there are at least three that clearly *refer* (italics mine) to the Rapture and several that are less plain."[5] The three basic passages are John 14:1-3; 1 Thessalonians 4:13-18 and 1 Corinthians 15:51-58. Others he mentions are 1 Thessalonians 1:8-10, 5:9-10; Revelation 4:1-2 and Titus 2:13. He also admits that the word Rapture is not found in the Greek New Testament.[6] Most scholars believe that the theory of a pretribulation Rapture was really not introduced until about 1830 with the teaching of John Darby. Scholars who have studied carefully their beliefs have rejected the attempts by LaHaye, Hal Lindsey and others to argue that early church Fathers like Justin Martyr, Irenaeus, Tertullian and others hold to their view of premillennialism. Although some of these writers were premillennialists, they did not subscribe to the modern dispensationalists' beliefs like a pretribulation Rapture or the radical distinction of the Jews being God's earthly people and the Christians as the heavenly people. They believed that all believers, Jews and others were the New Israel.[7]

## BEAM ME UP

Ben Witherington III has described LaHaye's Rapture theology as a "Beam me up, Scotty" (from the old Star Trek TV movies) belief that all Christians will be raptured to heaven and avoid the tribulation. This concept, Witherington notes, claims to be based on portions of the New

---

4. LaHaye, *The Rapture*, 77.
5. Ibid.
6. Ibid., 30.
7. Olson, "Five Myths About the Rapture," 4-5. See also Witherington, *Revelation*, 260-64.

Testament, "but their biblical interpretations are unwarranted."[8] Gary DeMar, a conservation scholar who has studied several of the novels and LaHaye's theology carefully, challenges LaHaye's conclusion by observing that "there is no single verse in the entire Bible that supports a pre-Trib. Rapture."[9] DeMar goes even further to note that "LaHaye and Jenkins have written a multivolume series to fill in events that the Bible nowhere discusses in relation to those and other supposed pretrib Rapture passages,"[10] referring in particular to 1 Corinthians 15 and Matthew 13:24–30 that the writers claim to employ.

In a telephone conversation with Dr. Craig S. Keener, Professor of New Testament at Eastern Baptist Theological Seminary and the author of a recent commentary on Revelation, published by Zondervan Press, I asked his opinion about the theology on which the *Left Behind* series was based. "Even though the *Left Behind* series may have some value for evangelism, if it preaches the saving Gospel, the biblical exegesis for the primary ideas about the end times," he observed, "are quite weak. I would guess that only a very small fraction of biblical scholars would think otherwise. I think that even most dispensationalists' scholars, of whom I am not one, would not be impressed with the biblical understanding behind the series."[11]

In an inquiry directed to Dr. Craig Blomberg, Distinguished Professor of New Testament at Denver Conservative Baptist Seminary, about his appraisal of the adequacy of the biblical foundation of the *Left Behind* series, he responded to me by noting: "I don't go so far as some former SBC moderates I knew did to call pretribulationism heretical though sadly, LaHaye thinks post-tribulationism is! But while premillennialism clearly appeared, at times even appeared to be the majority view, in the pre-Augustinian period of the church, there is no unambiguous evidence for pretribulationism until the work of J. Nelson Darby ca. 1830 and the foundation of the Plymouth Brethren Church. So while I leave the door open for it to be a possible biblical interpretation and thus not one that Christians should divide fellowship over, I do find it exegetically very weak."[12] Carl E. Olson, in his book, *Will Catholics Be "Left Behind?"*

---

8. Witherington, "What the Left Behind Series Left Out," 10.
9. DeMar, *End Times Fiction*, 17.
10. Ibid., 29.
11. Personal telephone conversation with Craig S. Keener on November 15, 2004.
12. Personal email from Craig Blomberg on November 16, 2004.

concludes that, "although many biblical references are used to support it, the pre-Tribulation Rapture has no basis in Scripture."[13] On his web site, Olson presses home more strongly his view about the fictional accounts as a whole. "The pretribulation Rapture dispensationalism, and the *Left Behind* books, in the end, are long on promises and short on biblical, historical and theological evidence."[14]

## A LACK OF BIBLICAL SUPPORT

William E. Hull, former Dean and Professor of New Testament at the Southern Baptist Theological Seminary in Louisville, Kentucky and Research Professor at Samford University in Birmingham, Alabama, stated at the 2004 Cooperative Baptist Fellowship's General Assembly in Birmingham, Alabama that the concept of the rapture that is LaHaye's centerpiece for his novels is not found in the Bible.[15] In an article published several years ago, Hull observed that although LaHaye likes to claim 318 scriptural references to the Second Coming and twenty-six rapture passages, "His whole effort to split the Final Advent into two parts separated by seven years is just not supported by these texts themselves."[16] He notes that there may be vague allusions to some kind of rapture but not enough to build a foundation for a theological superstructure.[17]

Mitchell G. Reddish, in his valuable commentary, observes that "in fact, nowhere in Revelation can the idea of a 'rapture' be found," nor does he think it can be supported in 1 Thessalonians 4:17 either.[18] In his commentary on Revelation, Ben Witherington III challenges and rebuffs the Dispensationalist's view of the Rapture, two second comings, two peoples of God or "about the saints being taken suddenly into heaven."[19]

Hal Lindsey, whose book, *The Late Great Planet Earth*, which I mentioned in chapter 2, also argues for a pretribulation view of the Rapture. He made numerous predictions about the end but had to acknowledge that

---

13. Olson, *Will Catholics Be "Left Behind,"* 290.
14. Olson, "Five Myths About the Rapture," 6–7.
15. "Samford professor delves into books, film in CFB General Assembly Workshops."
16. Hull, "Left Behind," 5.
17. Ibid.
18. Reddish, *Revelation*, 375, 387.
19. Witherington, *Revelation*, 260–62.

"the truth of the matter is that neither a post-, mid-, or pre-Tribulationist can point to any single verse that clearly says the Rapture will occur before the middle of or after the Tribulation."[20] Barbara R. Rossing, who made reference to Lindsey's quote above, observed that "the reason he is unable to point to a single biblical verse clarifying the Rapture chronology is that the Rapture itself is an *invented idea*."[21] (Italics mine).

## QUESTIONS TO PONDER

If the pretribulation Rapture concept is so essential to understanding the Scriptures, why did it take almost nineteen centuries for someone, namely Darby, to "discover" it? Why is there no clear mention of it in the Scriptures, the early Church Fathers, the Apostles' Creed, and the other creeds and confessions of the early church? Why did the General Assembly of the Presbyterian Church in 2001, the Lutheran Missouri Synod, Roman Catholics and others overwhelmingly approve resolutions saying that the Left Behind theology was not a sound biblical concept nor in accord with their denominational understanding of the New Testament? Why is it that even the fundamentalists differ widely on their interpretation of a fabricated pre-tribulation Rapture notion? The biblical scholar, James Barr, in referring to the "invention" of the Rapture, observes that this "'remarkable achievement of the mythopoeia fantasy' is a feat of the imagination worthy of the English poet William Blake."[22] It is indeed, and we should acknowledge that fact.

Many readers are not aware that Tim LaHaye, the biblical intellect behind the writings, is a rigid fundamentalist. He served as a member of the original board of directors of the Moral Majority and is now serving as the chair of the recently reactivated Moral Majority under its new name, "Faith and Values Coalition".[23] He is also an organizer of the Council for National Policy, which ABC News has designated as "the most powerful conservative organization in America." He has previously written books on the Rapture, one of them published under three different titles: *No Fear of the Storm, Rapture Under Attack* and *The Rapture*. He speaks often at Liberty University, Jerry Falwell's school, and keeps a close connection

---

20. Lindsey, *The Rapture*, 37.
21. Rossing, *The Rapture Exposed*, 36.
22. Quoted in Marty, "Year of the Locust," 47.
23. "Falwell creates new 'values' coalition," 3.

with Dallas Theological Seminary, probably the most conservative seminary in the United States. This is mentioned to remind the readers of the ultra conservative agenda behind these writings about being left behind.

## LAHAYE'S BIBLICAL CLAIMS

Let's look at a few of the chief biblical references which LaHaye claims support his pretribulation view of the Rapture and maybe we can see why biblical scholars do not support LaHaye's Rapture theories. LaHaye claims that most evangelicals support his views. This, however, is not the case. LaHaye does have support from some fundamentalists, especially those connected with Liberty University and Dallas Theological Seminary.

### 1 Thessalonians 4:13–18

> But we do not want you to be uniformed, brothers and sisters, about those who have died, so that you may not grieve, as others do who have no hope. For since we believe that Jesus died and rose again, even so, through Jesus, God will bring with him those who have died. For this we declare to you by the word of the Lord, that we who are alive, who are left until the coming of the Lord, will by no means precede those who have died. For the Lord himself, with a cry of command, with the archangel's call and with the sound of God's trumpet, will descend from heaven, and the dead in Christ will rise first. Then we who are alive, who are left, will be caught up in the clouds together with them to meet the Lord in the air; and so we will be with the Lord forever. Therefore encourage one another with these words. (The New Revised Standard Version).

LaHaye and other dispensationalists list this passage as the primary source for their pretrib Rapture belief. Note the following observations: (1) The chief emphasis of this passage focuses on the resurrection of Christ, not on some theory about believers being raptured into heaven. It clearly states the opposite view than the one proposed by LaHaye's interpretation. The passage states that believers will join Christ in the sky as he returns to earth, not heaven. This passage argues that there is only one coming in view, and that it's the same coming as the one mentioned in 1Corinthians 12: 35–56 that speaks of the trumpet, the link to the resurrection of Jesus and the future resurrection body. (2) The dispensationalists teach that Jesus' coming at the Rapture will be a secret and silent event, but this passage describes a very public event with the sound of God's trumpet, the Lord descending with a "shouted command" and a "call" from the archangel. Rather than quiet and secret, this coming will be the opposite with visibility and tumult.

(3) Paul wrote this letter to comfort the Thessalonians who were afraid that their loved ones, who were believers and had already died, would miss Christ when he returned. Paul was writing to assure them that those who had died would not be left behind but they would join Christians who were alive to meet Christ in the sky in a glorified body. Again Paul is stressing the opposite view of those who take the pretribulation Rapture view. (4) The passage also does not teach that after both of these groups, those dead and the present living believers meet Christ in the air, he will reverse his course and not go to earth but to heaven as the dispensationalists assert. This notion of a raptured church is not found in this text.

(5) This passage cannot be used to claim that Christ will return twice. There is no mention of this in the text. (6) The concept of "meeting the Lord in the air" draws upon what N. T. Wright calls an image of an emperor or some dignitary visiting a colony or province and the citizens go out to meet him and then escort him into their city. After the Christians "meet the Lord in the air," they will return with him to the transformed earth where he will reign.[24] The emperor does not, like the dispensationalists claim, change directions and return to where he came from. (7) The basic teaching of this text does not have anything to do with a concept of a pretribulation Rapture but addresses the believers' resurrection from the dead when Christ comes again. "What this letter is emphasizing is not that some will be left behind," Rossing insists, "but rather that we will all be *together* (italics hers) with our loved ones in our resurrection life."[25]

### 1 Corinthians 15:51–57

> Listen! I will unfold a mystery: we shall not all die, but we shall be changed in a flash in the twinkling of an eye, at the last trumpet-call. For the trumpet will sound, and the dead will rise immortal, and we shall be changed. This perishable being must be clothed with the imperishable and what is mortal must be clothed with immortality, then the saying of Scripture will come true: "Death is swallowed up; victory is won!" "O Death where is your victory? O

---

24. Wright, "Farewell to the Rapture," 8. See also Reddish, *Revelation*, 378 and Witherington, *Revelation*, 261.

25. Rossing, *The Rapture Exposed*, 175.

> Death, where is your sting? The sting of death is sin and sin gains its power from the law; but, God be praised, he gives us the victory through our Lord Jesus Christ (The New English Bible).

In the *Left Behind* novels this passage from 1 Corinthians 15:15–57 is the text that Pastor Vernon Billings of New Hope Village Church cites on his prerecorded videotaped message which he left for those who were left behind after so many persons had disappeared from the earth. This prerecorded tape by Pastor Billings is used to explain what happened to all those who vanished "in the twinkling of an eye." To the shocked and frightened persons who did not disappear, the pastor declares that Christ has raptured his church and he wants to give them instructions on what they should do next.

> Let me show you from the Bible exactly what has happened. You won't need this proof by now, because you will have experienced the most shocking events of history. But as this tape was made beforehand and I am confident that I will be gone, ask yourself, how did he know? Here's how, from 1 Corinthians 15:51–57.[26]

This passage like the 1 Thessalonians text is concerned with the general resurrection of the Christian and makes no mention of Christ rapturing the Church from the earth. (1) Again it is not a quiet or secret occurrence but happens with the sound of a trumpet. (2) The emphasis is on the transformation of the Christian's earthly body when it is raised from the dead into a spiritual one—from perishable to imperishable and from mortal to immortality. (3) The power of death is overcome in the victory of Christ's resurrection. 1 Corinthians 15 has as its central focus the victory of Christ's resurrection. Paul was writing to assure the Corinthians that there would be a resurrection from the dead. "But if it is preached that Christ has been raised from the dead," Paul argues, "how can some of you say that there is no resurrection of the dead? . . . If Christ has not been raised, your faith is futile; you are still in your sins. Then those also who have fallen asleep (died) in Christ are lost . . . But Christ has indeed been raised from the dead . . . " (1 Cor. 15:12, 17, 18, 20). With a strong affirmation about the resurrection of Christ, Paul then declares what the resurrected body will be like (1 Cor. 15:35–56).

(4) There is no mention in this passage about the Rapture, the Great tribulation, two comings of Christ, the antichrist or anyone being left be-

---

26. LaHaye and Jenkins, *Left Behind*, 209.

hind. This passage instead stresses the reality of Christ's resurrection as the foundation stone on which the believers, who may have died, have for their own resurrection when Christ comes again. All of Paul's metaphors in Corinthians and Thessalonians about trumpets, Christ in the air, the twinkling of an eye, shouts, etc. are not to be taken literally but seen as animated allusions to the marvelous transformation the Christian will experience in the resurrection. These texts are among the favorite passages that are read at funeral services. They are read not to point to some distant Rapture but to assure family and friends of the spiritual state that a believer has when he or she dies with faith in the living Lord.

*John 14: 1–4*

> Set your troubled hearts at rest. Trust in God always; trust in me. There are many dwelling-places in my Father's house; if it were not so I should have told you; for I am going there on purpose to prepare a place for you. And if I go and prepare a place for you, I shall come again and receive you to myself, so that where I am you may be also; and my way there is known to you. (The New English Bible).

LaHaye and other dispensationalists like to use this text as a reference to Jesus' own words to verify their Rapture views. (1) The references in this passage like "I am going there," "and if I go," and "I shall come again" may refer to Jesus' coming to his disciples following his resurrection or to his coming to them when the spirit has been poured upon them and he has been glorified or maybe to his coming at the close of history. (2) Some have seen this passage as a reference to the general resurrection of the Christians that both the Corinthian and Thessalonian texts address. (3) The reference to "prepare a place for you" is most likely a reference not so much to a future place but as assurance of a place of fellowship with him after his death and resurrection. "The central concern of the disciples in the larger context," William Hull suggests, "is not with where they will go after death but with whether they will be left alone on earth after Jesus departs to the Father."[27] This word is a word of reassurance and comfort to the disciples that they will not be abandoned. Rather they will draw strength from the risen Christ whose presence will be made manifest through the coming of God's Spirit (John 14: 16–18, 25–28). He will always be present with them (Matt 28:20). Jesus is not off and away in

---

27. Hull, *John*, 334.

heaven, distant from them, but is a present reality with them in the present moment and in the moments to come. "Where I am you may be also" is a strong assurance of identity and presence with them now. This is not a view of snatching them out of this world and taking them some place else but of making them aware of one who is already available. (4) This seems also to be the thrust of "receive you to myself" as a friend or relative welcomes another into intimate fellowship with them. The "rooms", "dwelling-places", "mansions", "household" or "resting places" are where the Christian already "abides" when he or she is in Christ. "And this is eternal life," John writes, "that they may know you, the only true God, and Jesus Christ whom you have sent" (John 17:3). John 14 is a reference not so much about a future happening but is about a present spiritual relationship one now has with Christ. It, of course, will continue beyond death, but it begins and continues throughout the course of one's life on this earth.

(5) The emphasis on the abiding presence of an intimate, personal fellowship with Christ today does not detract from the assurance of our being with Christ in our spiritual home after death. It should be a greater sense of confidence for a future hope when we can affirm a present sense of fellowship with Christ now. So this passage can still be properly used at funeral services. (6) Note a later reference in this passage, "I will not leave you as orphans; I will come to you" (John 14: 18 NIV). This seems to refer to an earthly appearance, after the resurrection, not to a heavenly one. (7) In John 5:28–29 it is predicted that Jesus will raise all the dead at the same time, some to be rewarded and some to be condemned. This would seem to rule out an earlier partial resurrection of only the Christians. (8) Again there is no support for two comings of Christ, seven years of tribulation following a Rapture, no reference to persons being left behind or to the Antichrist.

*Matthew 24:39–42*

> The flood came and swept them all away; so too will be the coming of the Son of Man. Two men will be in the field; one will be taken and the other left. Two women will be grinding meal together; one will be taken and one will be left. Keep awake, therefore, for you do not know on what day your Lord is coming. (NRSV).

LaHaye and others use this passage to try to support their pretribulation Rapture theory. This passage does refer to one person being taken and another being left behind, but it does not state that those who are taken are the believers and those left behind are the unbelievers. Dispensationalists have made that assumption but it is not in the text. New Testament scholar, N. T. Wright, sees this passage as one that focuses on persons who are taken "in judgment." He describes it as depicting those who might be like secret police who come in the night and seize all they can in a raid on a village. Rather than seeing those who were taken as a good sign, he interprets this passage in the opposite manner. Those who are left behind are the ones who were not captured in the judgment sweep and, therefore, they are the fortunate ones.[28] This passage is not clear on which is the preferred state of the two, those taken or the ones left behind. LaHaye assumes he knows. But those who lived under the Roman power knew the meaning of this passage, and I expect they thought to escape the terrorists and to be left behind was the better experience.

When one examines these texts which LaHaye claims are his best evidence for his pretribulation Rapture, the only logical solution one can reach is that they are wholly inadequate to support his claims. In many cases the texts actually assert the opposite view than the one he advocates. Not even a long stretch of the imagination can justify his claims. I am sure that a careful examination of the other texts he uses to support his theory really are dealing with other matters such as the resurrection of Jesus, Christ's final coming at the end of history, the Roman rulers in the first century or other clearly apparent persons or issues rather than a Rapture and about those left behind. If LaHaye's concept of the Rapture is invalid, which I have tried to indicate that it is, then the whole foundation for his novels is fiction as well.

## A SINGLE *PAROUSIA*

The New Testament clearly teaches only a single *parousia* or coming of Jesus again. The words, Second Coming, are not New Testament words. The common term used to describe the return of Christ is *parousia* which means "presence" or "appearing." This concept was drawn from an Old Testament concept of the "Day of the Lord." In the Hebrew mind this view denoted two ages, the present sinful age and the future age when

---

28. Wright, *Jesus and the Victory of God*, 366.

God would usher in the golden age when sin, suffering and death would be no more. This day was also a day of judgment on sinful humanity. Paul obviously linked the Day of the Lord and the *parousia*. The passage in 1 Thessalonians 4:13–5:11 is a vivid example of this teaching.

It seems clear from this passage that the Thessalonians thought that Christ was going to return in their own life-time. They were greatly troubled that some of the believers had died before he returned, and they were afraid that this meant that they would miss out on his return and not be a part of the new age kingdom which Christ would usher in. In this passage Paul is both teacher and pastor, theologian and counselor. This apocalyptic text is filled with symbolism and poetic images.

First, Paul offers them assurance and hope. Those who have died, he assures them, are only "asleep" and will join those who are still alive when our Lord returns. Their belief was evidently so strong that none of the believers would die before the return of Christ that the death of fellow Christians challenged their faith and their basic assurance in the resurrection of the dead. Paul assures them that the Christian hope is founded on Christ's victory over death through his resurrection. Second, Paul affirms his faith that the resurrection of the believers is based on the fact that Christ died and arose from the dead. He reminds them of something that is already known to them. "We believe that . . . " Paul is trying to help them remember what they already know and believe. Those who are alive when Christ returns, and Paul seemed to imply that he expected to be one of those alive then, will have no precedence over those who may have already died. Here Paul stresses his basic belief in the centrality of the resurrection of Christ as foundational for the believer's own assurance of resurrection and in hope for life beyond death.

Third, as a pastor Paul offers comfort to those who were grieving and thinking that their friends and loved ones would not experience the return of Christ because they had already died. He comforted them with the reminder that even if a person is dead, he or she still belongs to Christ and will rise when Christ returns. The Christian's relationship with Christ is not severed by death but continues. There is no mention of a Rapture or of a delay for those alive or dead when Christ returns. All will meet him together and at the same time. The poetic or symbolic use of the "shout" or "command" and the sound of the "trumpet" attest to the fact that no one will be unaware of it or will be "able" to sleep through the return of Christ. Both the living and dead will be aware of his *parousia*.

Fourth, Paul reminds the Thessalonians that no one knows when Christ will return. His return will be like "a thief in the night" (5:2). This phrase has unfortunately been used by dispensationalists to try and depict the return of Christ as a secret appearing. The basic thrust of this text, however, is to note that no one, including end times preachers and writers, can predict when our Lord will return. This passage attests to the fact that the coming of Christ also brings judgment for those who choose to dwell in the darkness instead of the light of the Christian way. "Paul's apocalyptic diction is not innocuous. It is radical and impinges on the quality of life lived in the present," Abraham Smith reminds us. "In many ways, it is reminiscent of the apocalyptic spirit found in the Negro spirituals. Although the spirituals were noted for their otherworldly orientation, they also had this-worldly functions."[29] The difficulties and struggles of this world, the darkness of evil and the mystery of death, especially the death of believers, created anxiety and uncertainty in the lives of Christians. Although the believers longed for the return of Christ, Paul cautioned them that they had no knowledge when the *parousia* would happen, so they were urged to be ready. This passage teaches that a belief in the resurrection of Christ is essential, Paul asserts, not some fictional concept of a Rapture as dispensationalists project.

Paul's discussion of the *parousia* in 1Corinthians 15: 1–58 is not about some kind of Rapture but about the final resurrection and the great Christian assurance that death is vanquished and the believer is freed from death's most radical claim. Drawing on the analogy of a seed, Paul notes that just as a seed is dissolved when it is planted in the earth and rises in a new form, so the earthly body of the Christian will be dissolved (changed) to rise in a spiritual body. Paul's central emphasis in this great passage focuses on the resurrection of the Christians at the return of Christ. He speaks about a "before" and "after" in the Christian's body. The two states might be depicted as follows: the present body is perishable, dishonored, weak and physical; while the spiritual body is imperishable, glorified, powerful and spiritual. Everything is reversed in the spiritual state. The new Adam, Christ, has through his resurrection brought this about. Paul concludes with an admonition for the believer to remain "steadfast and immovable" in the resurrection faith he has given to them (1Cor.15:1–5).

---

29. Smith, "The First Letter to the Thessalonians," 728.

*Discerning the Truth*  83

In an inquiry from me about his opinion on the dispensationalist's view of the Rapture which persons like LaHaye teach, Richard Vinson, former Dean and Professor of New Testament at the Baptist Theological Seminary at Richmond, Virginia and who teaches a course on Revelation, gave me the following response:

> The Rapture is the notion that Jesus, contrary to all New Testament teaching and to the understanding common to all Christian interpreters prior to the 1800's, will come to spirit away his followers just before the great tribulation begins. The New Testament very clearly and consistently teaches that Jesus will return once, at the last trumpet, in order to raise the dead in Christ (1Cor 15:23–24), to transform living Christians into forms more appropriate for eternity (1Cor 15:52), and to destroy every enemy of God (1Cor 15:24). Jesus' resurrection is called the "first fruits" of the general resurrection (1Cor 15:20), so that the resurrection of believers is the completion of the process begun when God raised Jesus; a secret rapture would be unconnected to the resurrection of Jesus, a theological anomaly. Jesus teaches his followers to be alert, prepared to endure the suffering of the tribulation, prepared to avoid the great deception (Mark 13:14–23). Had Jesus believed in the Rapture, he would not have said, "False messiahs and false prophets will appear and produce signs and omens, to lead astray, if possible the elect. But be alert; I have already told you everything" (Mark 13:22–23). Instead, he would have said something like, "False messiahs and false prophets will appear, but you won't have to worry about it, because you'll be in Heaven."[30]

## OTHER MAJOR PROBLEM AREAS

There are other problems with LaHaye's biblical interpretation that need to be addressed as well. Having spent some needed emphasis examining his Rapture views, we turn now and look at several other areas.

### *A Literal Interpretation of Scripture*

LaHaye has claimed that his basic approach to the Scriptures is "the Golden Rule of Biblical Interpretation." He believes that to depart from this rule often leads to confusion and sometimes even to heresy. Here is his Golden Rule. "When the plain sense of the Scripture makes common sense, seek

---

30. Personal email from Richard Vinson on November 14, 2004.

no other sense, but take every word at its primary, literal meaning unless the facts of the immediate context clearly indicate otherwise."[31] He is bold to assert that "anyone who follows the golden rule of interpretation will become a premillennialist."[32]

The sad truth is that most of LaHaye's invalid interpretations are based on his literalistic view of the Scripture. He not only takes passages literally that often should be read as symbolic, but he frequently lifts Scriptures out of their context and strings them together to try to force his own interpretation. "Misunderstandings of the nature of the imagery and the way it conveys meaning accounts for many misinterpretations of Revelation," Richard Bauckham observes in his book, *The Theology of the Book of Revelation*, "even by careful and learned modern scholars."[33] LaHaye is certainly guilty of totally misunderstanding and abusing the images from the Book of Revelation. In much of the *Left Behind* fiction, images are drawn from Revelation and then whole novels are constructed around the literal interpretation of the coming of the Antichrist, the mark of the beast, the time of tribulation, the desecration of the temple, the seals and plagues, the two witnesses in Jerusalem, Armageddon, the glorious appearing, etc. LaHaye has accused those who have wanted to interpret prophecy symbolically as bringing "confusion to the church."[34] Yet LaHaye often makes some strange choices when he chooses to draw symbolical interpretations on his own. In his *Glorious Appearing* novel, Jesus returns on a real white horse (Rev 19:11), but the "sharp sword" that comes out of Jesus' mouth (Rev 19:15) is taken symbolically (which, of course, it should be). In the *Glorious Appearing* Chaim Rosenzweig refers to the sword mentioned in Revelation 1:16, 2:16, 19:15 and 19:21 and links it to Hebrews 4:12 which says the "word of God" is sharper than any two-edged sword.

> "Now let me clarify. I do not believe the Son of God is going to sit on His horse in the clouds with a gigantic sword hanging from his mouth. He is not going to shake His head and slay the millions of Armageddon troops with it. This is clearly a symbolic reference, and if you are a student of the Bible, you know what is meant by a sharp, double-edged sword.

31. LaHaye, *The Rapture*, 238.
32. Ibid.
33. Bauckham, *The Theology of the Book of Revelation*, 22.
34. LaHaye and Jenkins, *Are We Living in the End Times?*, 6.

> "Hebrews 4:12 says the Word of God 'is living and powerful, and sharper than any two-edged-sword, piercing even to the division of soul and spirit, and of joints and marrow, and is a discerner of the thoughts and intents of the heart.'"

> "The weapon our Lord and Messiah will use to win the battle and slay the enemy? The Word of God itself! And while the reference to it as a sword may be symbolic, I hold that the description of the result of it is literal. The Word of God is sharp and powerful enough to slay the enemy, literally, tearing them asunder."[35]

When Christ appears on the literal white horse, he begins to quote Scripture, mostly in the King James Version, and his words mow the soldiers of Nicolae Carpathia down like they are being shot with a rapid repeating machine gun. Rayford is thrilled by the words but horrified by the carnage that comes from them.[36] LaHaye has Christ coming in glory and his words destroy those who were not believers and had the "mark of the beast". The impact of these words is described as follows:

> And with those very first words, tens of thousands of Unity Army soldiers fell dead, simply dropping where they stood, their bodies ripped open, blood pooling in great masses. "I am He who lives, and was dead, and behold, I am alive forevermore. Amen. And I have the keys of Hades and of Death."[37]

The sword may be symbolic but the horrifying images of the destructive force of the words are taken literally. Jesus is literally destroying those who did not believe in him. We will examine this theology later, but the novel paints the earth red with the blood of those who were not on Christ's side in the final battle. Armageddon, of course, is depicted as a real battle with Jesus literally defeating the armies of the Antichrist. Christopher C. Rowland reminds us that "Revelation offers a vision of another path of humanity than of the road of violence and evil."[38] It is interesting to note that in his own commentary on Revelation, LaHaye does not hesitate to pick and choose what is literal and what is not. "The red horse is obviously a *symbol* of war" (Italics mine),[39] the black horse a

35. LaHaye and Jenkins, *Glorious Appearing*, 192.
36. Ibid., 239.
37. Ibid., 204.
38. Rowland, "The Book of Revelation," 701.
39. LaHaye, *Revelation Unveiled*, 144.

symbol of famine, the pale horse, death, while the "beast that comes out of the sea" symbolized *obviously* (his word, the italics mine) the Antichrist and his kingdom."[40] The Sun-clothed woman was symbolic of "a great and wondrous sign."[41] The seven churches were seen as literal churches but also as representing the seven basic divisions of church history, a typical dispensationalist view.[42] And there are others.

LaHaye decides what is literal or symbolic mostly according to how it fits into his "Darby and Scofield's" view of the Scriptures. "Fundamentalists, then are not literalists, or not consistent literalists," James Barr, the renowned Old Testament scholars observes. "One could say that a main problem confronting a fundamentalists exegete is that of deciding which passages or which elements in the passage, he will take literally and which he will not."[43] This is certainly the dilemma that has confronted LaHaye. This leads us to our next problem, which arises out of this one.

### The Nature of Apocalyptic Literature

LaHaye has really denied the nature of the Book of Revelation and other apocalyptic literature in the New Testament by pressing upon them a wooden literalism. Apocalyptic literature, especially Revelation, is rich with symbols, visions, signs, poetic and figurative language, and any attempt to reduce it to some simple propositional statements is to miss its meaning entirely. The Book of Revelation is not some secret code to be deciphered but is conveyed in pictorial images that were painted on the minds of listeners as the original first century believers heard John's pastoral "letter" read to them as they gathered in worship. The images stirred their imagination and gave them comfort and encouragement. This symbolic message pointed through these images to the Christ who ultimately would be triumphant. To ignore the type of writing that apocalyptic literature is, will result in a misreading and distorted view of its message.

### Overlooking the People to Whom It Was Written

By turning the Book of Revelation into a book that is primarily about predictions concerned with the distant future would have made it mean-

---

40. Ibid., 143–44.
41. Ibid., 198.
42. Ibid., 35.
43. Barr, *Fundamentalism*, 47.

ingless to the original recipients in the first century. When LaHaye, Lindsey and other dispensationalists identify Babylon the Prostitute from Revelation 17 as the Roman Catholic Church, or the ecumenical church unity, or Russia, or modern Iraq, etc., they turn the Book of Revelation into a soothsaying manual about what would happen two thousand years after the book was written. "Revelation does not predict a sequence of events, as though it were history written in advance," warns Richard Bauckham, a renowned New Testament scholar. "Such a misunderstanding of the book cannot survive a serious and sensitive study of its imagery."[44] Biblical prophecy does not equate prediction. This approach tries to find the "secret code" in the images and visions of Revelation and crack the code and reveal all the futuristic predictions hidden in the book. Like other prophetic books of the Bible, such as Amos, Micah, Hosea, Jonah, Jeremiah, Isaiah and others, Revelation is a prophetic book in the rich meaning of the prophet's responsibility to preach God's word to his own people to call them sometimes to repentance and justice because of their sins and unfaithfulness to God and, at the same time, to affirm God's faithfulness, love, mercy and justice.

The prophet's word comes as a warning of what the consequence will be if people do not turn from their sinful ways. At the same time, the prophet offers hope to his listeners, if they will heed God's call. In Revelation the prophetic word is sounded to alert the people to God's judgment on the forces of evil and a summons to the believer to remain faithful and be assured of God's ultimate victory over injustice and terrifying circumstances. The prophetic word is both summons and hope, warning and promise, denunciations and encouragement, a call for repentance and reassurance of grace. The end time preachers have tried to turn the message of the Book of Revelation into specific events that will happen several thousand years later in the future and these events have already been determined and cannot be changed. This would not only "bind" God's hands and offer no opportunity, but, worst of all; it would not be a message that would help the people in the first century to whom John wrote originally to offer guidance and hope.

---

44. Bauckham, *The Theology of the Book of Revelation*, 149–150.

## The Seven Churches in Revelation

One of the strangest interpretations LaHaye and other dispensationalists make is their understanding of the seven churches in Asia to whom John sent his message. The seven churches are clearly named: Ephesus, Smyrna, Pergamum, Thyatira, Sardis, Philadelphia and Laodicea (Rev 1:11). LaHaye freely acknowledges in his commentary on Revelation that "obviously these were literal churches with which John was familiar."[45] LaHaye asks and then answers his own question about why were these particular churches selected. "It is suggested," he observes but doesn't say by whom, maybe Darby and Scofield, "that they also represent the seven basic divisions of church history."[46] Here LaHaye violates his own "Golden Rule" of interpretation. It is interesting that dispensationalists will accuse those who do not take the Apocalyptic Scriptures literally as "allegorizing" or "spiritualizing" prophecy. They charge them of "looking for some deeper 'secret' meaning other than the literal message conveyed by the words on the page" and one is forced to "invent any kind of 'Interpretation' you want."[47] But this passage about the seven churches (Rev 2:1–3:22) is a place where LaHaye and other dispensationalists have allegorized, spiritualized and "read into" the text what they wanted to insert there. It is a part of the myth and folklore of dispensationalism, but it is not found in the Scriptures.

Gary DeMar cites an observation from William Hendriksen, a New Testament Greek scholar, about the dispensationalist's effort to construct seven historical stages of nineteen hundred years from the seven churches in Revelation. Hendriksen calls this "interpretation" not only deplorable but also humorous. He continues with this striking observation:

> It should be clear to every student of Scripture that there is not one atom of evidence in all the sacred writings which in any way corroborates this thoroughly arbitrary method of cutting up the history of the Church and assigning the resulting pieces to the respective epistles of Revelation 2 and 3.[48]

LaHaye has read into Revelation whatever he needed to try and state his argument for a pretribulation Rapture. He cites Revelation 4:1–2 as

---

45. LaHaye, *Revelation Unveiled*, 35.
46. Ibid.
47. Hitchcock and Ice, *The Truth Behind Left Behind*, 7.
48. Quoted in DeMar, *End Times Fiction*, 30.

*Discerning the Truth*   89

the supposed Rapture of the church. This text, however, is not about the church but John's temporary "visit" to heaven. DeMar, who has carefully examined LaHaye's justification for this strange view of the seven churches, concludes, "LaHaye's thesis is based on his unproven assumption that Revelation 2–3 covers 'the church age using seven historical churches to describe the entire age.'"[49] As to the central concept of LaHaye's *Left Behind* fiction, the Rapture, DeMar is bold to declare, "Once again we are left wondering how the keystone doctrine of *Left Behind* is not found in the most comprehensive prophetic book in the Bible"(Revelation).[50]

### An Historical Time Out from Daniel

Another strange interpretation is the one that LaHaye uses to establish his basis for the seven-year period of Tribulation in the *Left Behind* novels. Of all places in the Bible, LaHaye selects several verses from Daniel to support his tribulation theory. One in particular is the following: "He shall make a firm league with the mighty for one week; and, the week half spent, he shall put a stop to sacrifice and offering" (Dan. 9:27 New English Bible). In keeping with Darby and other dispensationalists, LaHaye bases his concept of the tribulation from the discussion in Daniel 9:24–27 about seventy "weeks" of Israel's history. A week represents a year. This theory traces biblical history from the exile in Babylon to the Millennium. Biblical history is divided into seven sevens, sixty-two sevens, and one final seven.

Darby claimed that the first 483 years of Daniel's prophecy had been fulfilled up to week sixty-nine. When Jesus was crucified, according to this theory, God had to call a "time out" for prophetic history, because the Jews had rejected Jesus as the Messiah and Daniel's time table had to stop one "week" short. So, for two thousand years there has been a "time out" waiting for God to rapture the true believers and sit in motion once again the final "week" or seven years of the history of Israel. At the Rapture, dispensationalists claim, God will cause biblical time to begin again. These seven years following the Rapture will fulfill Daniel's prophecy as the count down on the final "week"—seven years of tribulation—begins.

This is a very brief digest of the most elaborate system one can imagine that is built around this selected passage from Daniel. LaHaye also claims to draw his seven years from Revelation 11:2 where two periods

---

49. Ibid., 31.
50. Ibid., 33.

of time he says are measured here.[51] By some wild math and isegesis, he reads into the text what he wants to find, not what the "plain texts" says.[52] He violates again his own Golden Rule of interpretation. It is also interesting that the Book of Revelation is filled with references to seven: seven churches (1:4), seven stars (1:16), seven candlesticks (2:1), seven seals (6:1), seven trumpets (8:6), seven heads (12:3), seven angels (15:1), seven bowls (16:1), seven kings (17:10), seven plagues (21:9), seven mountains (17:9), seven kings (17:10) and others. But there is no mention of seven years in Revelation. If this belief in seven years of tribulation is so critical to their theory and central to their *Left Behind* novels, why is there no reference to it in the main apocalyptic book that they have as a source? Few thinking persons can accept or follow this distorted use and abuse of Scripture.

> At the famed Wall, the two witnesses wailed the truth. At the tops of their voices, the sound carrying to the far reaches of the Temple Mount and beyond, they called out the news: "*Thus begins the terrible week of the Lord!*" The seven-year "week" had begun. The Tribulation.[53]

## A MORE VALID APPROACH

In chapter three we examined several ways that persons have interpreted apocalyptic literature. Those mentioned included: the spiritual or allegorical, the past-tense or the contemporary-historical, predicting for the remote future or the continuous historical, the end-times are coming soon or futurists, the political-religious typology, the dramatic-literary, and the apocalyptic view. Some of these approaches contain helpful ways of trying to understand apocalyptic literature, while others obviously either ignore the nature of apocalyptic literature or they use reproachful means of genuinely interpreting Scripture, especially the Apocalypse of John. We have examined some of LaHaye's and other futurist's abuse of Scripture in their interpretations, let me now propose which approach I believe is a more substantial interpretation of apocalyptic literature.

I favor the last one I mentioned in chapter four, the Apocalyptic approach. I have found this particular terminology, the apocalyptic in-

---

51. LaHaye and Jenkins, *Are We Living in the End Times?*, 151ff. See also LaHaye, *Revelation Unveiled*, 132–40.

52. LaHaye, *Revelation Unveiled*, 135ff.

53. LaHaye and Jenkins, *Tribulation Force*, 374.

terpretation, in the commentaries of several New Testament scholars, notably Kenneth H. Maahs and Julian Price Love.[54] Others have employed the same approach but have not used this title in their interpretation. This approach uses much that is good in some of the other interpretations but seeks to avoid the abuses of others. I am not going to repeat what was said in chapter 3 so you may want to refer to that discussion again. Here I want to list briefly some of the chief characteristics of this interpretation.

### It Takes Apocalyptic Literature Seriously

The Apocalyptic interpretation seeks to understand and treat the literary genre of apocalyptic literature. The Book of Revelation is not like other books in the New Testament and its special genre has to be considered carefully. Someone following this approach will study such books as John Collins, *The Apocalyptic Imagination* or Mitchell Reddish (editor) *Apocalyptic Literature: A Reader* or examine some articles in Bible dictionaries on apocalyptic writings and the Apocalypse and introductions to Revelation that give a detailed study of the literary genre of an apocalypse. As one examines the Book of Revelation, he or she is apprised by Collins to look for eight clusters of motifs in apocalyptic writings. (1) There is an urgent expectation of the end of earthly conditions in the immediate future. (2) The end will happen as a cosmic catastrophe. (3) The writing has a strong note of periodization and determinism. (4) Angels and demons have an active role in the writing. (5) There is an assurance of a new kind of salvation coming. (6) The Kingdom of God will be manifested in vivid ways. (7) A mediator with royal functions will play a central role. (8) The word glory will have a significant place. Collins, who drew upon Klaus Koch's suggestions here, reminds us that not all of these motifs will be in all apocalyptic writings.[55]

The cosmic conflict, the strange and sometimes startling images and figures, both human and animal, the other-worldly figures like the Son of Man, angels, Antichrist, the beast, demons, judgment, heaven and hell and the various numbers, etc. are understood as a part of a special literary technique to bring encouragement, reassurance and a call for fidelity to the persons to whom it was written, who were facing crises and persecution. Understanding the nature of apocalyptic literature, the

---

54. Maahs, *Of Angels, Beasts and Plagues*, 26–27; Love, "Revelation to John," 48.
55. Collins, *The Apocalyptic Imagination*, 12.

interpreter takes the images, visions, figures seriously but not literally. All symbols, colors, figures, numbers, persons, animals, time and geography have theological meaning. Unfortunately, much of the apocalyptic symbols just mentioned are lifted from their literary genre and placed in the *Left Behind* novels as an abuse of their original intention by the author of Revelation. In his book on Revelation, *Approaching Hoofbeats: the Four Horsemen of the Apocalypse*, Billy Graham alerts his readers to the fact that the author, John, was an apocalyptist. "That is, he wrote Revelation in a certain type of poetic language known as apocalyptic languages . . . that used vivid imagery and symbolism to speak about God's judgment and the end of the world."[56]

### *It Takes the Time in Which Revelation Was Written Seriously*

Any serious attempt to understand the Book of Revelation cannot ignore the people or the time in which it was written. To take the meaning of the Apocalypse as the futurists do and see it as a book about some predictions that will happen some two thousand years later takes all value away for the believers in the first century to whom it was addressed originally. If we are going to understand Revelation, we will have to read it in the context of other Jewish apocalyptic literature of its own day. A part of the interpreter's responsibility is to determine to the best of one's ability the social, political historical, ethical, literary and theological setting of the book. "The primary rule to follow in interpreting such literature is," according to Ben Witherington III, "*what it meant to the original audience is still what it means today*" (Italics his).[57]

### *It Takes Seriously the Crisis of Its Own Day*

Rather than focusing on some crisis that the futurists like LaHaye do that will happen two thousand years later, the apocalyptic interpretation views the book as written to speak to the crisis the early church was encountering under the Roman persecution of Christians in the first century. To see the book predicting some crisis with the pope, Russia, modern Iraq, modern Israel or the world Council of Churches denies its meaning for the people of its own day. Before we can find any meaning for us today, the interpreter must recognize why and to whom the book was written in

---

56. Graham, *Approaching Hoofbeats*, 22.
57. Witherington, "What the Left Behind Series Left Out," 52.

the first place. When we are able to grasp that knowledge and understand why and how it addressed the first century Christians, then we can try to discern its message for us today as believers.

### *It Takes Symbolism Seriously*

Understanding the nature of apocalyptic literature, the interpreter knows the significance and rich meaning of the use of symbolism in Revelation. The interpreter knows that to take this symbolism literally is to turn the book into something that it was never meant to be. Much nonsense and strange, far fetched historical and international projections have come from futurists like LaHaye, Lindsey and others who have identified some person, place or time as fulfilling the prophetic meaning of Revelation only to have to change that prediction after that person died or a country like Russia was no longer a threat or some new leader came unexpectedly on the horizon.

The *Left Behind* novels are constructed on the false premise of literalism. To turn symbols like "the mark of the beast," "the two witnesses," the outpouring of the bowls of judgment, the visions of the trumpets, the plagues of wrath, Babylon, the Antichrist, Armageddon, etc. literally may be entertaining like science fiction or action or spy thrillers but theologically and biblically they communicate a distorted concept about God, Christ, the power of sin and evil, the church, redemption and most other historic Christian doctrines.

Literalism does not help people understand Revelation better but misinforms them and distorts their ability to grasp its real meaning. To ignore or miss the powerful symbolism of Revelation and transcribe it into a literalistic form can cause us actually to miss the real meaning the Apocalypse has for us today. When we really understand what the symbolism originally meant then we discover their meaning in a similar way for our generation today.

### *It Takes Seriously Biblical Scholarship*

Those who use the apocalyptic interpretation use the best tools of critical biblical scholarship to understand and interpret the Book of Revelation. The reader is not frightened by scholarship but acknowledges that it helps open the way for a realistic and valid interpretation of the Apocalypse. Good biblical scholarship opens up the ancient world to the interpreter so he or she can grasp what the writer was saying to the persons to whom he was writing. It examines the literary genre, the Greek language in which it was written, the apocalyptic symbolism, the social, political, cultural and religious climate of its day, how Revelation is understood with other apocalyptic literature of its own day and those written earlier, the relationship of Revelation to the other New Testament and Old Testament writings, and other areas of thought.

This approach is seeking the truth about the Apocalypse and not reading it with preconceived notions of what it is saying. It does not confine itself to a "prison" of literalism, which would prohibit it from discovering the real meaning of the rich imagery and symbolism of this dramatic and poetical-like book. It affirms that we follow Christ who is the truth and who seeks to lead us into a deeper and fuller knowledge of all things. It is not fearful of scholarship but embraces it in its quest to know the truth that sets us free. It seeks to draw insights into understanding Revelation from any source or discipline, religious or secular that will offer meaningful guidance into the literary genre of the Apocalypse.

### *It Takes Seriously the Book As Prophecy*

The apocalyptic approach affirms that Revelation is a prophetic book in the proper sense of that word as a "forth-teller" not a "fore-teller". The Book of Revelation is not primarily a book foretelling or predicting future events thousands of years beyond its own time, which would have no meaning or significance to the people to whom it was written, but it is a book of prophecy which proclaims God's word to the people then. A prophet brings a warning about the pending judgment of God and a call for repentance. The prophet also issues a summons for faithfulness from believers during the crisis and suffering and assures them of God's presence, faithfulness and ultimate victory. The prophet first of all addresses the people to whom it was written with a ringing call for fidelity and a reminder of the certain judgment of God on the powers of evil. It served as a helpful word for them then and was not some projection about things to happen in some remote time in the far distant future. John was a true prophet who believed that God was still involved in the history of the world and his sovereign way would in the end defeat the way of wickedness and evil.

Although John, the Seer, was not directly addressing our time, his message is still one that can communicate God's word to us today. The Apocalypse sought to revive the hope of the Christian believers during a time of danger and crisis. Its message of hope still addresses the believers wherever dangers and difficulties threaten. As we discern how John spoke to the believers in the first century, we can in turn see how his words speak to similar conditions and needs in our own day. In that sense, John's prophecy can still be a word from God for us today as well.

*It Takes the Application of Revelation Seriously*

Once we understand what the message of the Apocalypse was for its original readers in the first century and sense its message through its rich symbolism, then we seek in a similar kind of way to discern, sense, intuit its message for our generation. What does it say to us? As we struggle with our present day demons and beasts of terrorism, famine, pollution, AIDS, racism and sexism and countless others, we discover the presence of the Christ who encourages us as believers and passes judgment on the evil doers and assures us of the ultimate triumph of good over evil.

A proper awareness of the socio-political situation in the first century and how the Christians then confronted their adversaries offers us guidance in how to meet the enemy in our own day. The battle between good and evil continues. It is a perpetual struggle. The monsters, beasts, symbols and scenes may change but the struggle is the same and our resources to combat them are the same as those of the believers in the first century—the omnipotent presence and power of the Eternal Christ who ultimately will be victorious. We are still challenged to be faithful until the end as the first century Christians were. The rich symbolism of the early church's struggle against the powers of tyranny and suffering create meaning for us in the present moment. Our identification with these brave Christians in the past gives us strength and direction in our world today. Kenneth H. Maahs notes how Revelation is meaningful today in the following:

> The apocalyptic approach also recognizes Revelation as a manual for contemporary holy war. Here is how the church is meant to deal with the overwhelming forces arrayed against it. Revelation is not just a description of the first century—which would say little to us—nor is it merely a sketch of the final generation—which may not involve us either; rather it is a portrayal of life here and now, as

we are living it. Its first century context is a transparency, a looking glass, through which we are able to see our own world, which might already be in its final phase. Thus, there are symbols in the book that stand for *us!* We must start to live them![58]

This chapter has attempted to show the reader that the hermeneutic that underlies LaHaye and Jenkins's novels is inadequate and not based on sound biblical scholarship. His basic themes of the pretribulation Rapture, seven years of tribulation, a secret return of Christ, and his literalistic understanding of Scripture cannot be supported by sound biblical scholarship. I have cited only a few of many respected scholars who find the novels void of solid biblical insights. Most biblical scholars do not subscribe to LaHaye and Jenkins's interpretation and many actually find them dangerous and harmful to a genuine understanding of Christian doctrine. I personally believe that the biblical interpretation set forth in the novels is as fictional as the novels themselves. LaHaye's inadequate biblical view is not the only way of understanding the Bible. I have suggested that one will find a richer and more meaningful approach by following an apocalyptic interpretation of Revelation. Our quest after all is to discern the truth, isn't it? Let's continue that quest!

---

58. Maahs, *Of Angels, Beasts and Plagues*, 27.

6

# Critiquing the Theology Behind the *Left Behind* Novels

IF OVER SIXTY-TWO MILLION persons have read or at least purchased a copy of some or all of the *Left Behind* novels, there has to be some reason for their blockbuster success. Many persons are intrigued with the mystery of life, the fear of death and the end, and the puzzlement of the Book of Revelation. Tim LaHaye and Jerry Jenkins have touched that nerve of special interest and have invited readers to travel with them to the uncertainty of a certain end time. They have built tense, suspenseful apocalyptic thrillers around a special "Mission Impossible Team" called the Tribulation Force. This group of daring persons is formed after Jesus (according to this belief) has raptured the church from this world and unbelievers are left behind. New believers arise and compose this courageous group and the reader is summoned to follow them rescue other believers and Jews from the enemy lines, fool the enemy and beguile the enemy and divert his equipment and supplies for their own usage.

The action thrillers are filled with murders, executions, daring escapades, romance stories, personal conflicts, a touch of science fiction, skirmishes with military police, special forces on the land and in the air, intriguing ways of outwitting the enemy and a struggle to come to grips with a strong faith. Although the novels are not great literature, they are easy to follow. And they offer hope, if not always succeeding, for those who are longing for a word of hope in a confused world. LaHaye claims that these stories are based on a valid interpretation of the Scriptures, especially the Book of Revelation. Those who read these stories of fiction may tend to believe that they are indeed biblical themselves and contain some authority that is not rightfully theirs. To declare that these novels are books of fiction is one thing but to assert that the theological interpretation behind these novels is the only valid one is troublesome. "If the interpretive methodology set forth in the series is embraced as the Biblical method," Gary DeMar concludes, "then I believe many people will be disappointed and disillusioned when the scenario outlined by LaHaye does not come to pass."[1]

Many people have been confused and some even frightened by the theology of the *Left Behind* novels. To me, the confusion and fears go beyond the concept that the end might be coming soon and we might not be ready for it. Their basic concepts about God, Christ, salvation, conversion, hope and others in the fiction writings offer very un-satisfying and distorted images of these beliefs. In the last chapter we examined the biblical terminology in the *Left Behind* novels about Rapture, the literal interpretation of Scripture, the nature of apocalyptic literature the seven churches in Revelation, the "timeout" in Daniel, etc. and found that these interpretations by LaHaye and Jenkins cannot be supported by a sound interpretation of the Scriptures. Few New Testament scholars support these pretribulation claims, and they also dismiss their instance on taking apocalyptic literature literally as a misunderstanding and abuse of the kind of literature it is. We will build on the conclusions from the last chapter as we examine the theology behind the *Left Behind* novels. Since LaHaye has never been reluctant to offer his criticism of others with whom he differed, I offer my critique of the end times fiction.

## GOD

I must begin by saying that I find the view of God in the novels very unsettling and disturbing. At times I find it difficult to understand how God's actions differ from the despicable and capricious acts which the antichrist figure, Nicolae Carpathia does. They both issue out undeserved suffering on persons who either did not recognize who they were or were undecided about their loyalty. Suffering from the sting of the demon locusts God had sent, Dr. Chaim Rosenzweig, Jewish Noble Prize-winning Israeli Botanist and statesman, cries out in agony, "Why would God do this to me? What did I ever do to him?"[2] Here Buck confronts Chaim with his sin of pride. Several times when the question is raised about why God permits such awful suffering and pain, the response that is given is that

---

1. DeMar, *End Times Fiction*, 207.
2. LaHaye and Jenkins, *Apollyon*, 322.

this is God's final way of trying "to get the attention" of the unbelievers. When some of the plagues are sent to torment the people, many of them already had the mark of the beast and could not repent. So, the punishment would have to be vindictive and punitive.

Many persons, including Rayford and Chloe, often asked why God sent or permitted so much suffering on the unbelievers. "Daddy, what does this make God? Some sick, sadistic dictator?" Chloe asked her father after he explained how he thought God had raptured the church and left the rest behind to respond to God's call for repentance. "You think I'm wrong, but what if I'm right?" Rayford counters." Then God is spiteful, hateful, mean," Chloe responds "Who wants to go to heaven with a God like that?"[3] When Rayford was listening to Pastor Vernon Billings' tape about the Rapture, he hears the pastor's response to those who might wonder why God would rapture his church and bring such shock and despair to those left behind. He reminds his listeners that this is God's judgment on an ungodly world. This period of trial and tribulation will give those left behind another chance. "This is God's final effort to get the attention of every person who has ignored or rejected him," Billings declares.[4]

What kind of God would send such awful suffering on people "to get their attention?" Does God send cancer, heart attacks, accidents, war, AIDS and other calamities to get our attention so we will believe? This would equate God with the Antichrist that comes to afflict others. Only an inadequate and pagan notion of God would depict God as vindictive, revengeful and deliberately sending suffering, accidents and other forms of pain. To take the images from Revelation literally and see them as God's way of judging unbelievers or non Christian humanity with suffering and pain "to get their attention" or to punish them is a distorted concept of the God revealed in Jesus Christ.

Rather than being a demonic and hateful God, Jesus has revealed to us a God of love and grace. The small epistle of First John gives us one of the highest insights into God's nature. "God is love" (1John 4:8, 16). Love is at the very center of God's being, and everything God does is consistent with the divine nature of love. The New Testament reveals that God is not angry with human kind but loves them. "For God so loved the world that he gave his only son so that everyone who believes in him may

---

3. LaHaye and Jenkins, *Left Behind*, 165.
4. Ibid., 212.

not perish but may have eternal life" (John 3:16). God, like the shepherd seeking the lost sheep in one of Jesus' parables, reaches out in love to the whole world and longs for its redemption. God's love is not manipulative or coercive but seeks to draw persons to God's presence out of love. Jesus said, "And when I am lifted up from the earth, I will draw all people to myself" (John 12:32). This is the magnetic power of love. God doesn't use demonic creatures to get our attention or punish us. The good news of the gospel about God is the depth of God's love for humanity revealed in the cross of Christ. "God commended his own love toward us, in that while we were sinners, Christ died for us" (Rom. 5:8). God does not want to punish us or destroy us but longs to restore any broken relationship between us. God reaches out to us in love not hate. Our knowledge of love arises because "God first loved us" (1John 4:19).

Writing in one of his books published after the series of the *Left Behind* novels was released, LaHaye stated: "I must declare that I cannot view God as a cruel taskmaster, standing at the gate of heaven to keep people out. Instead I see him as the loving, merciful heavenly Father"[5] That is a wonderful statement. I wish this concept about God were revealed in the novels he and Jenkins wrote. But it is not. In this end times fiction God is capricious not loving, malignant not merciful. The Book of Revelation assures its readers of the loving providence of God. God's love will continue to be faithful because all of history is under God's sovereignty. God is driving history to its final goal and believers can be assured of God's loving and abiding faithfulness even in the midst of suffering and persecution. The God who is forever faithful calls upon the believer to remain faithful and continue to trust in God's presence and mercy.

## JESUS CHRIST

The Book of Revelation opens with the centrality of Jesus Christ. "The revelation of Jesus Christ, which God gave him to show his servants what must soon take place" (Rev 1:1 NRSV). The chief focus of the book is not on some end times events to take place thousands of years later in the history of humanity, but stresses the role of "the Lamb of God" as the power and presence of God in confronting the powers of evil which the first-century believers were experiencing. In chapter five of Revelation the Lamb is first introduced as the one who is able to open the book with

---

5. LaHaye with Halliday, *The Merciful God of Prophecy*, xiv.

its seven seals. In this dramatic moment in the Book of Revelation the Lamb is called "the Lion of the tribe of Judah" and "the Root of David," both messianic titles. He is described as still bearing the marks of having been slain in sacrifice, yet having "seven horns," omnipotent power, and "seven eyes" which depict the "all seeing omniscience of God. This figure is, of course, not to be taken literally but is symbolic of the limitless power and all knowing and limitless presence of Christ.

In the Gospel of John, John the Baptist described Jesus as "the Lamb of God who takes away the sins of the world" (John 1:9, 36). Peter states that we were ransomed "with the precious blood of Christ like that of a lamb without defect or blemish" (1Pet. 1:19 RSV). The root of this image goes back to the Old Testament, but the Lamb of God was not the usual metaphor used in the Old Testament to depict the Messiah. The typical images for the Messiah were shepherd, ruler, lion, and especially king. John had read Isaiah and some of the other prophets who noted that the Messiah was to be the Lamb of God, a suffering servant. His image was drawn from the deep spiritual well of the fifty-third chapter of Isaiah. We read these words:

> He was despised, he shrank from the sight of men, tormented and humbled by suffering: we despised him, we held him of no account, a thing from which men turned away their eyes. Yet on himself he bore our sufferings, our torments he endured, while we counted him smitten by God, struck down by disease and mercy; but he was pierced for our transgressions, tortured for our iniquities, the chastisement he bore is health for us and by his scourging we are healed" (Isa. 53:3–5).

The fifty-third chapter of Isaiah is one of the great passages in the Old Testament about the Suffering Servant. To whom does this passage refer? Some have seen it as a depiction of the suffering of the nation of Israel. Others have seen it as a collective figure for one or several of the great Jewish prophets. Without question the New Testament writers saw it as a prophecy of Jesus Christ, the One who laid down his life on the cross. The Lamb in Isaiah's image stood before the shearers as the rejected and despised One, who laid down his life for others.

John's Gospel not only seems to draw upon the Suffering Servant figure of Jesus as the Lamb of God, but he utilizes the image of the Passover lamb as a reference to Jesus also. According to John's Gospel, the moment Jesus was crucified on the cross was exactly twelve noon (John 19:14).

This was the time that the lambs were sacrificed in the temple for the Passover. It seems that John is picturing Jesus as the Pascal lamb. Paul, in 1Corinthians 5:7, one of the earliest writings in the New Testament, declares: "Christ our Paschal Lamb has been sacrificed."

In the large stained glass window behind the pulpit in St Matthews Baptist Church in Louisville, Kentucky, where I served as pastor for ten years, there is an image of a lamb on the large cross. One Sunday one of our church members was sitting in the congregation with her granddaughter waiting for the service to begin. The small child looked at the lamb's image in the stained glass window and turned to her grandmother and exclaimed, "The lamb looks hurt." And indeed it is! The image of the lamb in that window is symbolic of the Lamb of God who laid down his life for us.

There is another picture of the Lamb in the Scriptures. In the Book of Revelation the word lamb is used twenty-nine times. The Lamb that was slain has now become sovereign; the Lamb that was victim has now become victor. This Lamb is depicted as a reigning, conquering figure. The "seven horns" symbolizing power and royalty, and the "seven eyes" signifying omniscience (Rev 5:6) denote the slaughtered Lamb as the conquering "Lion of Judah" which was a Jewish apocalyptic imagery.[6] The one who was slain is now victorious. He is the Lamb who saves the world from its sins.

The Greek word for lamb, which is used in Revelation, is different from the one used in the Gospel of John. William Barclay states that John's use of this new word for lamb in Revelation is a way of declaring that "this is a new picture and a completely new conception."[7] Here John has created a new symbol for a conquering figure. Rather than a fierce lion, the victorious Lamb "the faithful and true witness" (Rev 1:5), conquers non-violently by self-sacrifice. Instead of using military armies, the Lamb uses the power of sacrificial love. "Then I saw between the throne and the four living creatures and among the elders a Lamb standing as if it had been slaughtered" (Rev 1:6 NRSV).

John's theology of the Lamb undercuts one of the basic emphases of the *Left Behind* novels-the whole concept of a military "Tribulation Force" that uses weapons and force to confront their enemies and persecutors. The power of the Lamb is non-violent and "conquers" its enemies

---

6. Beasley-Murray, *The Book of Revelation*, 124–25.
7. Barclay, *The Revelation of John*, 216.

by love and sacrifice, not by force and coercion. LaHaye and Jenkins have completely misunderstood and distorted the image from revelation. The depiction of "the Lamb, who was slain" as one who seems to be punishing or taking revenge on those who killed him, totally misconstrues "the Suffering Servant" image. LaHaye and Jenkins use the scriptural words of Jesus (the sword in his mouth) to kill thousands of people. "And with those very first words," (scripture quotations about "the faithful witness" and "ruler over the kings of the earth," etc.), tens of thousands of Unity Army soldiers (the antichrist's army) fell dead, simply dropping where they stood, "their bodies ripped open blood pooling in great masses."[8] This interpretation is completely opposite of what John is trying to communicate about the Lamb and his followers. How can it possibly be reconciled with the concept of God "who so loved the world" and who sent his son to save the world? The concept of the Lamb who kills people is such a distortion of the image in Revelation that it is amazing!

I am convinced that John's reference to "a robe dipped in blood" (Rev 19:13) is in keeping with his theology of the sacrificial Lamb in whose blood Christians wash their garments and they are made white (Rev 7:14). M. Eugene Boring declares that "John's theology as a whole calls for this interpretation."[9] The blood is on the conquering Lamb's robe *before* he enters into battle. The bloodstained robe portrays the cross and suffering death of Christ. "In the Apocalypse, Christ conquers not by shedding the blood of his enemies," Mitchell G. Reddish, asserts, "but by shedding his own blood for his enemies."[10] Jacques Ellul, a noted theologian, reminds us that the only blood in this passage (Rev 19:13) is that on the Lamb whose victory comes through the sacrifice of the cross. "The robe dipped in blood is not different from the white robe of the first vision: it is not the blood of enemies," he maintains, "it is white by the purification obtained through the cross."[11] Brian K. Blount follows a similar argument when he states "that the Lamb is indeed noted for being slaughtered, not for slaughtering others . . . The blood on his robe is his own; he does after all, still bear the residue of slaughter." The "sharp sword" in his mouth, he observes, "is his cutting testimony of his own true Lordship. It represents

---

8. LaHaye and Jenkins, *Glorious Appearing*, 204.
9. Boring, *Revelation*, 196.
10. Reddish, *Revelation*, 368. See also Maahs, *Of Angels, Beasts and Plagues*, 246–47.
11. Ellul, *Apocalypse*, 109.

oppositional witness, not violent combat,"[12] G. B. Caird affirms that the only weapon the Lamb wields is his own cross and the martyrdom of his followers. (See Rev 2:27; 12:5; 19:15).[13] True to the theology throughout the rest of the Book of Revelation, the Lamb, even as a Lamb on a white horse, is still viewed as the "pierced one," "who was dead and now lives," and "the Lamb that was slain from the creation of the world" (Rev13:8 NIV).

## THE CHURCH OR COMMUNITY OF BELIEVERS

The Book of Revelation was originally written to strengthen and encourage the believers in the first century churches to remain faithful during the difficult time of persecution under the Roman government and to be assured of Christ's ultimate victory over the oppressing forces of evil. The message to the seven churches addressed their individual needs, giving both commendations and warnings when needed. Likewise, other churches then and now heard and can still hear the challenging message. The Lamb of God—Jesus Christ—is the central figure of Revelation and the model and guide for Christian believers. Revelation 14 pictures the community of true believers who have not submitted to the forces of evil and have remained faithful to the Lamb. The number 144,000 should not be taken literally but should be seen as representative of all the faithful believers or those who became martyrs for not committing spiritual adultery by worshipping the beast or false gods of the Roman Empire. The key verse is that the 144,000 (the whole company of true believers) "follow the Lamb wherever he goes" (Rev 14:4). The early Christian community is composed of those who "follow the Lamb." The Christian community takes its guidance and instruction from the Lamb. The One who said he had come to serve and not be served (Mark 10:45) and that the greatest of all is the servant of all (Matt 20:27) is the church's model and standard. As followers of the Lamb, we are not the assailants or enforcers, but we follow the One who has called us to minister and serve.

The notion of "the Tribulation Force", which LaHaye and Jenkins present in their novels, stands in opposition to the Book of Revelation's image of the followers of the Lamb. The Tribulation Force uses weapons of violence like hand guns and uzizes, planes and helicopters, Land Rovers and trucks that blow up armored carriers and kill soldiers and utilize some

---

12. Blount, "Wreaking Weakness," 296.
13. Caird, *The Revelation of St. John the Divine*, 293.

of the most advanced technological equipment one can have to combat the forces of the Antichrist. In the *Left Behind* novels the Tribulation Force begins to form as Buck joins Rayford, Chloe and Bruce Barnes as the fourth member. "Together these four have determined to stand and fight against all odds, to never give in . . . and Bruce Barnes knows from his study of Scripture that dark days lie ahead."[14] Unlike Revelation that speaks of the martyrdom of first century believers, *Left Behind* portrays a large underground, secret organization that takes on the Antichrist's forces and out maneuvers and outwits them on many occasions.

A central verse for understanding the meaning of "the conquering Lamb" of the Book of Revelation is found in Revelation 12:11. "But they have conquered him (Satan- the Antichrist) by the blood of the Lamb and by the word of their testimony for they did not cling to life even in the face of death." The community of believers is victorious over the powers of evil not by killing them and shedding their blood but through the "blood of the Lamb." This is a reference to Christ's death on the cross and to the victory over sin he achieved by his sacrifice. If we are followers of the Lamb, we identity our lives with the One whose blood was shed on the cross, and we take up our "cross" to follow him in his self-giving, servant hood model. Paul reminds us, "Let the same mind be in you that was in Christ Jesus, who though he was in the form of God did not regard equality with God as something to be exploited, but emptied himself taking the form of a slave . . . and became obedient to the point of death- even the death on a cross" (Phlm. 2: 5–8).

Unfortunately, most dispensationalists, like LaHaye, Hal Lindsey, Pat Robertson, Jerry Falwell, Jack Van Impe and others, advocate violence and war, which they try to draw from the image of the conquering Lamb in Revelation. As I have already stated, I believe that this is a total misreading of the image. The Christian conquers not by attacking others and spilling their blood but through the victory Christ has already achieved in the shedding of his own blood. The believer does not seek to inflict pain and suffering on one's enemies but seeks to help them realize that the cross of Christ has already won the battle. The video game, based on the *Left Behind* series, has been criticized for its violent content and its

---

14. LaHaye and Jenkins, *Tribulation Force*, ix.

emphasis on destroying or converting the non-Christian.[15] But the video game picks up the theme of violence from the novels themselves.

John reminded the believers in the first century that their enemies were conquered first of all through the shed blood of Jesus Christ the Lamb of God. Secondly, in verse 12:11, he states that they are conquerors over their enemies by their word of testimony "and their willingness to die for their faith." Their personal witness, akin to the two witnesses in chapter 11 in Revelation, communicates the reality of the faith within. Their willingness to lay down their lives to seal their testimony to their faith shows the genuine depth of their belief. By word and deed, their speech and life, courage and blood, they have borne witness to Christ and have followed in the conquering Lamb's way. Revelation assures us that though our enemy may spill the blood of believers, the ultimate victory has already been won by the Lamb who shed his own blood. The Lamb calls his followers to service, non-violence and love, not to hatred, violence and war. The *Left Behind* Tribulation Force in no way represents the teachings of Jesus who instructed his disciples to resist evil, not to cause it.

> You have heard that it was said, "An eye for an eye and a tooth for a tooth." But I say to you, Do not resist an evildoer. But if anyone strikes you on the right cheek, turn the other also; and if anyone wants to sue you and take your coat, give your cloak as well; and if anyone forces you to go one mile, go also the second mile. Give to everyone who begs from you, and do not refuse anyone who wants to borrow from you. You have heard that it was said, "You shall love your neighbor and hate your enemy." But I say to you, Love your enemies and pray for those who persecute you, so that you may be children of your Father in heaven (Matt 5:38–43 NRSV).

When Jesus was arrested in the Garden of Gethsemane, Peter drew his sword and cut off the ear of one of the soldiers. "Put your sword back into its place," Jesus said, "for all who take the sword will perish by the sword" (Matt 26:52). Here Jesus very pointedly spoke against using violence even for his own protection.

The Tribulation force of *Left Behind* has drawn its model from the *Pax Romana*, the military peace that uses violence, force, military buildups, weapons and intimidation to control people. The followers of the Lamb seek to establish the *Pax Christi*, which is built on justice, love, un-

---

15. "Video game for Christians draws criticism," *Richmond Times Dispatch*, December 12, 2006.

derstanding, mercy, hope and reconciliation. The community of faith, the Church, finds its model in the one who said, "Blessed are the peacemakers, for they will be called the children of God" (Matt5: 9).

## CONVERSION/ SALVATION

In the *Left Behind* novels a high priority is placed on evangelism and the conversion of selected individuals who are left behind. Rayford, Chloe, Buck, Pastor Barnes, Chaim Rossenzweig and several others have their conversion experience noted. Sometimes the focus is on inauthentic faith like Pastor Barnes, who was a minister at New Hope Village Church where Irene Steele, Rayford's wife, was a member. Barnes realized that his inauthentic faith caused him to be left behind. He confessed his problem.

> I thought I had a great life. I even went to Bible college. In church and at school, I said the right things and prayed in public and even encouraged people in their Christian lives. But I was still a sinner. I even said that. I told people I wasn't perfect; I was forgiven . . . . I had a real racket going . . . . And I bought into it. Down deep, way down deep, I knew better. I knew it was too good to be true. I knew that true Christians were known by what their lives produced and that I was producing nothing.[16]

His conversion is used as a model and as a catalyst to probe readers to examine their own faith. Barnes had been sincere in his faith to the point that neither his wife nor other people at church questioned his conversion. But deep down in his heart, he knew his faith was not real. Fundamentalists, like LaHaye, often challenge the sincerity of another person's faith unless they have gone through the "transaction" process that they think is essential for salvation. This usually entails confessing one's belief in a certain list of theological propositions. The time and place one was saved also needs to be known and shared with others.

After Barnes shared his testimony, he guided them through the "steps" to an authentic salvation. When Rayford and Chloe hesitated about responding then, he cautioned them: "If God impresses upon you that this is true, don't put it off. What would be worse than finally finding God and then dying without him because you waited too long?"[17] This fear tactic is used throughout the novels to try to force the unbeliever

---

16. LaHaye and Jenkins, *Left Behind*, 196.
17. Ibid., 203. See also LaHaye and Jenkins, *The Rapture*, 160, 215.

to respond. This is a common strategy of fundamentalists. Chloe, Buck, Rosenzweig and others are cautioned not to wait too late to respond. Hattie, Rosenzweig and several others have to endure some of the terrible plagues before they are finally converted. Both the fear of punishment and judgment and the dread of personal suffering are used as a means to lead persons to accept Christ. Again and again the phrase God's last chance "to get their attention" is used to justify the sending of the horrible suffering on unbelievers.

Most of the conversions of the central characters like Rayford, Chloe, Buck, Hattie, Ken, Mac, etc. take place in private and when they are alone. Others are told about them later. Rayford's conversion follows his viewing of the Rapture tape by Pastor Billings. "He was alone with his thoughts, alone with God, and he felt God's presence."[18] He kneels and prays the "sinner's prayer" of confession of sin and trusting in Christ. "If you were genuine," Pastor Billings continues on the tape, "you are saved, born again, a child of God."[19] Chloe's conversion takes place on an airplane, and Buck's in a washroom.[20] Bruce Barnes had described the salvation experience as a "transaction." This transaction views Jesus' death as bearing our sins and paying the penalty for our sins so we do not have to bear the costs. When we acknowledge our sins and receive Christ's gift of salvation, Barnes notes, Jesus saves us.[21] A clear distinction is made in the novels between those who are saved and the unsaved, believers and unbelievers. According to this understanding of conversion, after confessing one's sins, the sinner invites Jesus to come into his heart and it is at that moment one is saved. The novels use the word "transaction" to describe what has taken place in one's conversion experience, being born again or experiencing the new birth. I find transaction a strange, non-biblical word, to describe the salvation experience. Conversion is not a business negotiation but an encounter with the redeeming Lord, who opens up a new relationship with God through the forgiveness of our sins and the depth of God's grace and love.

In the *Left Behind* novels, immediately upon being converted, the believer receives a mark on one's forehead that is recognizable only to

---

18. Ibid., 215.
19. Ibid., 216.
20. Ibid., 406–9, 446–47.
21. Ibid., 200–1.

another believer. This, of course, gives them an absolute certainty about their conversion and visible proof that the new birth transaction has indeed transpired. This fantasy evidence raises serious questions about the meaning of faith and the need for "signs" to believe. This may cause some believers to question their own conversion because they have no "visible sign" of its reality. They may even question the depth of their own salvation experience as they check off the propositions one has to believe to be saved.

## EVANGELISM

### Opportunity for Evangelism

The writers of end times books often state that one of their chief goals in their works is to reach people for Christ before he returns. Some people were first introduced to the Gospel message by reading Hal Lindsey's, *Late Great Planet Earth*. I remember talking with college students who were not Christians and became interested in knowing about Christ after they got in a college group discussing Lindsey's book. Curiosity and some degree of apprehension had triggered their interest, not a religious quest. In a book, entitled *Are You Rapture Ready?* Todd Strondburg and Terry James discuss the signs, threats, prophesies, warnings and suspicions that note that "the end" is near. They make an evangelistic appeal when they write, "The best advice one can give is to repent now and avoid the panic and heartache later. The Rapture will indeed be the greatest *media event* ever."[22] (Italics mine). Adrian Rogers, a leading Southern Baptist minister in Memphis, Tennessee, extends his evangelistic message in a question and answer format in *Unveiling the End Times in Our Time*. "Do you want to be ready when Christ returns? The only way to do that is to receive the One who came and died on a cruel cross for the forgiveness of your sin and the salvation of your soul."[23] Pat Robertson also believes that the approaching return of Christ provides a special opportunity for Christians to witness. "This can be the greatest hour of evangelism the Christian Church has ever known."[24]

During the interview on *60 Minutes* II on April 4, 2004, LaHaye stated that many people had a "God hunger" today and by reading the *Left*

22. Strondberg and James, *Are You Rapture Ready?*, 126.
23. Rogers, *Unveiling the End Times in Our Time*, 11.
24. Robertson, *Bring It On*, 287

*Behind* books had come to faith and are evangelical Christians today.[25] One of the links on the *Left Behind* web site offers guidance in how one may become a Christian. Throughout the *Left Behind* novels in various circumstances, the "plan of salvation" is presented. Most of the time the way it is given is basically the "Roman Road" or a variation of it. First, they remind the person or persons that "all have sinned and fall short of the glory of God" (Rom. 3:23). Next, they would state that "God shows his love for us in that while we were yet sinners Christ died for us" (Rom. 5:8). Then they call for a response in Romans 10:9, "If you confess with your lips that Jesus is Lord and believe in your heart that God raised him from the dead, you will be saved."[26] Marilena Carpathia, the mother of Nicolae, the Antichrist, was witnessed to by three young people in the prequel, *The Rising*, who used the Roman Road plan to try and reach her for Christ. She, of course, rejected their efforts.[27] Chloe states in *Kingdom Come*, set in the Millennium, that "evangelism is what we're all about. It's why we're here."[28] This in fact is indeed an underlying theme in all the novels in one way or another.

### Instantaneous Conversions

In most cases the conversions to Christ take place instantaneously. Sometimes these conversions happened right before someone had to face the guillotine, and they responded to the witness of Chloe or someone else. Thousand of Jews are converted by the preaching of Tsion Ben-Judah in the Old City in Jerusalem as the massive army of Carpathia approached the city to destroy it in the Battle of Armageddon. The pressure was on to decide quickly or be damned forever. The idea that seven years of tribulation after the Rapture will lead to the conversion of unbelievers raises serious questions about evangelism and God.

No one can deny that conversions may sometimes happen in the first moment one hears the Gospel message. Saul on the Damascus Road would

---

25. This claim is also made in the "Author's Notes" in LaHaye and Jenkins, *The Rapture*, 348; and in LaHaye and Jenkins, the "Note from Dr. Tim LaHaye," in *Kingdom Come* in the 356.

26. LaHaye and Jenkins, *Left Behind*, 200ff. For another example see LaHaye and Jenkins *The Mark*, 223ff. See also LaHaye and Jenkins, *The Rapture*, 64, 82, 134, 215f.; and LaHaye and Jenkins *Kingdom Come*, 133, 230f, 303.

27. LaHaye and Jenkins, *The Rising*, 120–26.

28. LaHaye and Jenkins, *Kingdom Come*, 243.

be the classic example. However, few people are actually reached that way today. George G. Hunter, Professor of Church Growth and Evangelism at Asbury Theological Seminary in Wilmore, Kentucky and the author of several significant books on evangelism, notes that his "interview research with converts suggest that about thirty links are involved in the chain that leads to faith."[29] He acknowledges that this is an average that varies depending on how "far back" in the witnessing chain one goes.

Chloe, Rayford Steele's daughter, Buck Williams, who later became Chloe's husband, Dr. Chaim Rosenzweig and Hattie Durham take exceptions to the quick conversions. At first Rayford tries to pressure Chloe into making a decision but backs off and lets her respond at her own pace. Buck also responds in his own way slowly and thoughtfully to the teachings of Bruce Barnes, who became the "acting" pastor of New Hope Village Church after the Rapture. Since he was among those left behind, Bruce was converted himself after listening to his pastor's tapes predicting the Rapture. Rayford also tried to witness to Buck but realized he needed to let Buck, as he did Chloe, respond when he was ready. Buck's faith decision was made in the washroom of the United Nations Building as he prepared to go into a conference called by Carpathia. Rayford had come down the church aisle earlier at the New Hope Church following Bruce's sermon on the "Four Horses of the Apocalypse." He had talked with Bruce earlier and listened to the tape about the Rapture that the former pastor, who was one of those taken in the Rapture, had left to offer guidance to those who were left behind and what they needed to do to get right with God. Rayford and others witnessed several times to Hattie Durham, who had been the senior flight attendant on the 747 airplane with Rayford. She said she wanted to believe but did not think God could save someone like her. Most of the witnessing to individuals personally takes place in the first volume, *Left Behind*. Irene, Rayford's first wife who was taken in the Rapture, was converted alone after reading a brochure about salvation from a friend who had invited her to come visit her church, New Hope Village.[30]

## *Isolated Witnessing*

In the other volumes of the *Left Behind* series little witnessing, except for isolated instance is actually done by "The Tribulation Force", because

---

29. Hunter, *Radical Outreach*, 35.
30. LaHaye and Jenkins, *The Rising*, 376–379.

they remain hidden underground or are engaged in covert activities to help other Christians find safety or are busy learning about the plans of Carpathia, the Antichrist. Most of their evangelism was through the teaching or preaching to the cyber audience of more than a billion by Tsion Ben-Judah, the converted rabbinical scholar. It is difficult for Christians to witness if they remain isolated in their Christian ghettos. One can argue that these Christians had to hide, of course, to save their lives. That's true but you never read of any of them seeking out unbelievers to share the Gospel with them, except Ben-Judah who goes to the Jews in the Old City of Jerusalem before the final Battle of Armageddon begins.

*A Negative Response*

If the publishers of the series are correct in their research, only twenty percent of those who read the *Left Behind* novels are unbelievers. Has any study been done to see how many of these persons were converted by reading the novels? The kind of evangelism exhorted in these writing issues in a summons for an immediate and certain response without any real questions or reservations. In these novels there is often no real time to think seriously about who Jesus really is. You don't have time to think or reflect. You must respond before it is too late or you are killed. That kind of pressure will obviously force you to say, "I believe." But how can there be time to understand to whom or what you are giving your alliance?

Has any study been done to show how many persons are actually turned off by the evangelism concept and Rapture theology expounded in the novels? Initially, some people were drawn to the Gospel message by Hal Lindsey's book, *Late Great Planet Earth*, only later to acknowledge that they found his views flawed and they had difficulty believing in Christ at all because of their negative feelings about his book. How many readers of the *Left Behind* series would get in this same line and want their money back?

*The Church Is Rarely Involved*

Evangelism is important to our understanding of the Christian faith but the *Left Behind* novels have focused on a type of evangelism that takes place in isolation and without the support and instruction of the faith community—the Church. An exception to this is seen in the prequel, *The Regime*, where Irene tries to get her Rayford, Chloe and Raymie to go with her to the New Hope Village Church. However, it is a member of the church named Jackie who witnesses to Irene, but she attends the church only a few times and makes her commitment apart from the church itself.[31] Even the "reported" thousands of conversions that Tsion Ben-Judah has reached through the cyber-audience are still individual listeners to a preacher on TV. The church-community plays almost no role in reaching others for Christ. It is a one on one approach, with a call for a quick immediate response or one is lost forever. The fear of eternal damnation or of being left behind is used to try to get persons to make a quick decision for Christ. Leah Rose, a former nursing supervisor at a major hospital in Palatine, Illinois, described to Rayford what she had often been told when she delayed making a commitment to Christ. The following quote is what she says she was often told when she "floundered spiritually." This approach is used in the novels as a way of condemning those who want to raise questions about spiritual issues or to take some time to reflect on this commitment.

> Evangelists and evangelistic-minded friends had told her and told her that a nondecision was a "no" decision. She had argued. She wasn't saying no, she said; she was still thinking. Well, one of her well-meaning friends had said, don't think yourself into hell. Or into being left behind.[32]

### Fear Motive

The novels claim that the concept of the Rapture, especially the fear of being left behind, "may be the greatest evangelistic tool in human history."[33] The novels use the Rapture theme as an instrument to encourage unbelievers to decide so they won't be left behind. The novels show, however, that even those who are left behind following the Rapture still have a chance to be saved, if they will respond to the gospel message. All the novels are constructed around characters that have become Christians after the Rapture and become the Tribulation Force, and engage in various conflicts with those who oppose Christ's way.

One of the most unrealistic approaches to evangelism in the novels is the method used by Tsion Ben-Judah through cyber communication

---

31. LaHaye and Jenkins *The Regime*, 211ff.
32. LaHaye and Jenkins, *Glorious Appearing*, 352.
33. Hitchcock and Ice, *Left Behind*, 79.

to share the message with supposedly "millions" about the Rapture and what the judgments and punishments from God are going to be and why people should respond immediately to the gospel message. Again, the writers build on fear and press for decisions if persons are to avoid the suffering and the condition of being lost forever. Persons are urged to respond to a message that is mostly the quotation of various Scripture passages to "prove" that the biblical prophecy, which they are preaching, is true and is coming to pass. A meter on the cyber communications network indicated that tens of thousands had responded to Tsion's teaching and the numbers were rising. Rayford looked at the meter and thought that it was malfunctioning. The meter was racing so rapidly that he could not even see the individual numbers. "He sampled a few of the responses: Not only were many converted Jews claiming to be among the 144,000 witnesses, but Jews and Gentiles were also trusting Christ."[34]

When you think about it, what person would not want to respond to Christ when almost every day terrible plagues are affecting people that cause them pain, suffering, confusion, dread and awesome fear? Almost anyone would respond to avoid any more suffering. But this raises my original concern that I mentioned at the beginning of this chapter: What does this say about the "character" of God? It does not depict a God of love but one who wants to chastise, punish and make humanity suffer to respond to him. This picture reminds me of the pagan gods of Rome and Greece, not the God of love and grace that Jesus Christ revealed.

### ARE THE NOVELS EFFECTIVE EVANGELISTIC TOOLS?

LaHaye "estimates" that at least one hundred thousand readers have so far made a decision to receive Christ as their Savior through the influence of the novels.[35] He, of course, offers no evidence for this estimate. Amy Johnson Frykholm in her book, *Rapture Culture,* reports about numerous interviews she has had with readers of the *Left Behind* novels and found few who had been able to use the novels as effective tools for "witnessing" and few who had been converted by reading them. In a letter to her from Jerry Jenkins, he claimed to have received letters from 2,000 people who say they have accepted Christ because of the books.[36] In a response

---

34. LaHaye and Jenkins, *Soul Harvest*, 243, 245, 250.
35. LaHaye, *The Merciful God of Prophecy*, 11.
36. Frykholm, *Rapture Culture*, 164.

from Tyndale House Publisher when she inquired about persons who had actually been converted by the *Left Behind* novels, she received only seven letters, four reporting the conversion of someone else and only three who spoke about their own conversion. In all her research, she could not find anyone who said that he or she had become a Christian because of reading the novels. "As I conducted my research, I searched in vain for a person who could testify to a life changed through the reading of *Left Behind*."[37] Frykholm observes that Tyndale House has published a book that seeks to address this issue: *These Will Not Be Left Behind: Incredible Stories of Lives Transformed after Reading the Left behind Series* (Wheaton, IL. Tyndale House Publisher, 2003). This book gives excerpts from e-mails, message boards and letters. She notes, however, that these annotations are mostly told in the third person and the first person e-mails are one or two lines long. She concludes that the book rather than solving the problem only compounds it.[38]

One of the central problems with the type of evangelism that is presented in the novels, as I said earlier, is its insistence on instantaneous conversions. Sometimes persons take a short time to respond to the gospel message but the fear factor is always raised if they wait. George G. Hunter, whom I mentioned above as a Distinguished Professor of Church Growth and Evangelism at Asbury Theological Seminary and who has spent a lifetime practicing, teaching, and writing about evangelism, observes that the Willow Creek Community Church maintains that there is a "chain" of experiences that leads to faith. Rather than happening suddenly, Hunter concludes that there are usually about thirty links that are involved in the chain that leads to a valid religious experience.[39] This is the reason a faith community, the Church, is so important and essential in this process. Few persons ever become Christians in isolation. Authentic evangelism will show concern for the total person and will address the need for discipleship and the role of the Church in one's spiritual growth. One does not arrive at the time of conversion as a mature Christian. A lifetime of continuous growth lies before a new convert. I have tried to address some of these issues in my book, *Authentic Evangelism: Sharing the Good News With Sense and Sensitivity*.[40]

37. Ibid.
38. Ibid., 201.
39. Hunter, *Radical Outreach*, 35.
40. Tuck, *Authentic Evangelism*.

## RESURRECTION OR RAPTURE

The concept of the Rapture is a fictional account that LaHaye and other dispensationalists have manufactured to support their strange misreading of the Bible. Rather than the resurrection being central to the Christian faith, they have inserted this "invented" rapture doctrine as primary. Most of the New Testament Scriptures they use to try to support their rapture theory really focus on the resurrection of Jesus or on the Second Coming. In *Left Behind,* pastor Billings' tape, which he recorded before *the* Rapture, uses I Corinthians 15:15–57 as a proof text for the Rapture.[41] But this passage, as I indicated in the last chapter, is about the resurrection not the Rapture. The texts from 1 Thessalonians 4:13–18, John 14:1–4, Matthew 24:39–42, Titus 2:13 were examined briefly in the last chapter, and I stress again that their focus is either on the resurrection of Jesus or the Second coming. Dispensationalists claim that there are two future appearances of Jesus, one at the Rapture and the other at what they call the Glorious Appearing. But the New Testament speaks only of *one* Second Coming, not two.

Many do not realize that dispensationalists, like LaHaye, have replaced the resurrection belief with this fabricated Rapture concept. This cuts out the heart of the Christian faith. The resurrection is the foundation stone of the Christian faith. "Christianity stands or falls with the reality of the raising of Jesus from the dead," declares the noted theologian, Jurgen Moltmann. "In the New Testament there is no faith that does not start *a priori* with the resurrection."[42] It is "the sustaining foundation of the Christian faith," Wolfhart Pannenberg declares. "If this collapses, so does everything else which the Christian faith acknowledges."[43] For the apostle Paul nothing could displace or be substituted for the resurrection. "If Christ has not been raised," Paul asserts, "your faith is still futile and you are still in your sins" (1 Cor. 15:17). If the resurrection proved false, then our salvation, forgiveness, reconciliation and hope for eternal life-everything essential to our faith—collapses with it. To exchange the resurrection for the Rapture as LaHaye and other dispensationalists have done is not a minor tinkering with our religious beliefs but it is "literally" throwing the baby out with the bath water. It replaces the foundation stone

---

41. LaHaye and Jenkins, *Left Behind,* 209.
42. Moltmann, *Theology of Hope,* 165.
43. Pannenberg, *The Apostle's Creed in the Light of Today's Questions,* 97.

of the Christian faith with a fabricated non-biblical concept. "A Christian faith that is not resurrection faith," Moltmann affirms, "can therefore be called neither Christian nor faith."[44] In the light of Moltmann's claim, the question then needs to be raised, if LaHaye and Jenkins have substituted the Rapture concept for the resurrection belief, should these novels then be called Christian fiction?

If that criticism seems too harsh, note that LaHaye identifies Jesus' power to raise Lazarus from the dead, his claim that, "I am the resurrection and the life. He who believes in me, though he may die, he shall live. And whosoever lives and believes in me shall never die" (John 11:25–26), Paul's claim "to be absent from the body is to be present with the Lord" (2 Cor. 5:8) and other passages that deal with the resurrection and Second Coming—all these passages—as being pressed into his Rapture mold.[45] Then he makes a bold assertion, which clearly shows his substitution of the Rapture for the resurrection. "Christ is coming to resurrect and translate His church. We *call* that the Rapture" (Italics mine).[46]

The great creeds and confessions of faith all assert a belief in the resurrection of Christ and in his second coming, but I have never read any creed, confession or doctrinal statement of faith that speaks about the Rapture. The whole series of novels are based on a fictional doctrine, the Rapture. It was the resurrection of Jesus and not the Rapture that turned a defeated and despairing group of disciples into crusading evangelists for the gospel of Christ. It is the resurrection that sustains the Church for its battle against the forces of evil, because it assures us of a living, risen Lord, who is present with us today. It encourages us to live with confidence in the face of suffering, misunderstanding, persecution, rejection and death.

There are three great witnesses to the resurrection of Jesus Christ. The first is the Christian Church itself. The resurrection was what founded the Church. If Jesus had not been raised from the grave, there would never have been a church. The Church came into existence because of the disciples' belief in the risen Lord. The New Testament is the second greatest witness. The New Testament did not create the Church. Disciples in the early church wrote the Gospels, Acts, and the rest of the New Testament to tell others about Jesus Christ, the risen Lord. The third witness to the

---

44. Moltmann, *Theology of Hope*, 166.
45. LaHaye, *The Rapture*, 41.
46. Ibid.

reality of the resurrection is that the Jewish disciples changed their day of worship from Saturday—the Sabbath—to Sunday. As sacred a day as the Sabbath was to the Jews, only a miracle could make them change their day of worship from Saturday to Sunday. This miracle they declared was the resurrection of Jesus. If the crucifixion and death of Jesus were the end of his career and life, then neither the Church nor the New Testament would have come into existence. The resurrection made the difference!

## JUDGMENT

The *Left Behind* novels are filled with the judgments God releases on the unbelievers. LaHaye and Jenkins take all of the images in the Book of Revelation literally. People suffer miserably from the stings of locusts, water turning to blood, boils and sores on their bodies, earthquakes, blinding darkness, hail and fire raining down from heaven and all the rest. Barbara Rossing observes that "the *Left Behind* novels seem to suggest that God is largely removed from this earth, inflicting plagues and earthquakes on it . . . but otherwise living in heaven, waiting for the end of time."[47] Bruce Barnes introduced Rayford and others to the judgments to come:

> This period of history we're in right now will last for seven years. The first twenty-one months encompass what the Bible calls the seven Seal Judgments, or the Judgments of the Seven-Sealed Scroll. Then comes another twenty-one month period in which we will see the seven Trumpet Judgments. In the last forty-two months of these seven years of tribulation, if we have survived, we will endure the most severe tests, the seven Vial Judgments. That last half of the seven years is called the Great Tribulation . . . What are these judgments? They get progressively worse, and if I'm reading this right, they will be harder and harder to survive.[48]

The Tribulation Force and other believers are marked with a sign on their foreheads. They are exempted from the curses and plagues because of their beliefs. The judgments, as I mentioned earlier, are God's way, according to the *Left Behind* novels, of getting the attention of the unbelievers so he or she will accept Christ. Later after Nicolae Carpathia has been assassinated in Jerusalem and was resurrected at the G C Palace complex in New Babylon, which was televised for all to see, he declares himself divine and

---

47. Rossing, *The Rapture Exposed*, 11–12.
48. LaHaye and Jenkins, *Left Behind*, 309.

demands worship. Those who consent to worship Carpathia, who really is the Antichrist, are given a mark on their forehead. If anyone refuses this mark, that person is put to death. The persons, who bear the mark of the beast or are not yet believers in Christ, like Jews and others not having the mark, are the ones who suffer under the judgments of God.

Time and again throughout the novels the question is raised why a loving God would send such atrocities on people. Tsion, the converted rabbi and the primary teacher of Christianity, seeks to answer that question to his cyber audience.

> Many of you have written and asked me how I explain that a God of love and mercy could pour out such awful judgments upon the earth. God is more than a God of love and mercy. The Scriptures say that God is love, yes. But they also say he is holy, holy, holy. He is just. His love was expressed in the gift of his Son as the means of redemption. But if we reject this love gift, we fall under God's judgment.[49]

This depicts a vindictive God that demands allegiance and will give no one freedom not to respond without the fear of being punished. How does this differ from the demand of Carpathia, the Antichrist, that he be worshipped? Everyone was required to get the mark on their forehead or on their right hand as a sign they would worship Carpathia. Is this the dreaded 666? Without the mark people could not buy or sell. If they refused the mark, they were beheaded.[50] It would be hard to exist in that tyrannical community without that mark. That's the reason, of course, the Tribulation Force went underground and became covert in their operations to survive. LaHaye and Jenkins are clear that once someone got the mark, there was no turning back. The mark and decision was once and for all.

The finality of this decision in the novels is deeply troubling to me. Look at the picture: millions had witnessed by television or in person the resurrection of Carpathia, who had been assassinated and was lying dead in his casket. How many actually saw the risen Lord after his resurrection? We believe it by faith today. In these novels, millions actually saw Carpathia rise up from the dead. Why would they not think that he was divine? The mark was supposed to be a sign of worship and identity with him, but without that mark, people really could not exist- no food, no

---

49. LaHaye and Jenkins, *Assassins*, 175.
50. LaHaye and Jenkins, *The Mark*, 85.

work, no purchasing or selling. And without it, they would be killed. It is easy to see why they would take the mark. Who knows how many, if any had heard the gospel message. But how could they prove its truth? They had actually witnessed- actually seen—Carpathia come back to life. How were they to know that this was not an act of God instead of the work of Satan? Oh, I know, the Tribulation Force, or the few—Rayford, Bruce, Chloe, Buck- they knew from the Rapture tape from Pastor Billings. But others did not!

Persons who may never have had an opportunity to know about Christ and the gospel are condemned eternally because they sided with Carpathia and got his mark when they thought he was divine or they simply feared for their lives. What about the gospel teaching of Acts 2:21. "Everyone who calls upon the name of the Lord shall be saved." Or Romans 10:13. "For everyone who calls on the name of the Lord shall be saved." Or John 3:15. "Whoever believes in him may have eternal life." In conversation with Carpathia's secretary when Rayford had sneaked into Babylon during the siege of utter darkness from one of the judgments, the woman seems to want to free herself from the powers of the Antichrist. But Rayford knows that it is too late because she bears "the mark" of the beast.

Many, like this woman may have been willing to respond to God's grace when they finally knew the real evil nature of Carpathia. Who is to say that it is too late then? The Good Shepherd who goes after the one lost sheep would surely not shut the door on anyone who genuinely wanted to repent and be saved. To use the "mark" as if it were a clear conscious decision to choose the evil one over Christ seems to press that image too far. The novels show clearly that many factors went into taking the mark, and not necessarily a desire to worship the Antichrist at all. And even if someone began with that kind of adoration in the light of Carpathia's resurrection, maybe when his evil nature unfolded, they would turn away from him in disgust.

The *Left Behind* novels are filled with images of blood, mangled bodies, endless suffering, carnage and heinousness atrocities. When the words of Jesus destroy the unbelievers in his Glorious Appearing, the blood rises to four feet. The sword from Jesus' mouth- the Word of God- the Scriptures- slices through the air, reaping the wrath of God's final judgment upon them. Rayford declared that they had been given chance after chance and God sent all kinds of judgments to persuade them, but they would not respond. They were seeing "for the first time the One they had pierced," but "it was too late."[51] Suppose they had been able to "see" Jesus as they had Carpathia, would they not have believed? Why would they be brought to faith by a God who sent punishment upon them without their clearly understanding why it was happening? Rather than the "pierced" Lamb redeeming them by his blood, Christ is killing them and letting their blood flow. This is not the One who came to seek and to save the lost. Even in the novel about the Millennium, *Kingdom Come*, where Christians live to be a thousand years old, if an unbeliever does not accept Christ before he or she reaches a hundred, that person will be judged by God as unfaithful and die.[52] These unbelievers are called "The Other Light." Abdullah Ababneh, a Christian believer, comments to a neighbor about The Other Light, "But God exterminated one this morning."[53] The funeral service of a woman named Cendrillon, who died at a hundred without confessing Christ as Lord, is used as a warning to unbelievers of what will happen to them if they do not accept Christ before they reach this age even in the Millennium.[54]

Barrie Shepherd, in reflecting on the concept of judgment in the parable of the "five foolish maidens" who were late and found themselves shut out of the wedding feast, concludes his prayer on what seems such harsh judgment on them for their forgetfulness with these words of hope:

> One hope I find in all this:
> That, though I will be judged, my Judge
> will be the One who knew that stable birth,
> that dreadful cross, that liberated tomb; the One
> who healed and taught and embraced children,
> fed the hungry, even raised the dead.
> So, Lord, tonight I pray for all
> who are a little late or come with empty lamps,
> including me; that somehow, in your everlasting mercy,
> there may be a second sitting, or a spot beside the door
> where we can kneel and watch and catch a glimpse,
> share a song. In such a hope I lay me down tonight.
> Amen[55]

---

51. LaHaye and Jenkins, *Glorious Appearing*, 208. LaHaye also says in *The Merciful God of Prophecy*, 87 that "God is patient but he will not withhold his hand of judgment forever."

52. LaHaye and Jenkins, *Kingdom Come*, xiv, 58, 60, 248.

53. Ibid., 122. See also 182.

54. Ibid., 58.

55. Shepherd, *A Child Is Born*, 17.

One of the cardinal teachings of Jesus is about forgiveness. He is also the model and guide for forgiveness (Luke 11:4; 23:34). Our forgiveness is determined by God's patience (Mark 11:25). George Beasley-Murray has directed us to a deeper awareness of the parable of the Prodigal Son as a parable about the kingdom of God in the following lines:

> Traditionally it has associated the coming of the kingdom of God above all with judgment, and with connotations of condemnation at that. Yet here in the parable of the Prodigal Son Jesus presents the sovereignty of God in terms of a love that delights in restoring the wayward to the fellowship of love. Nor should we regard this emphasis as somehow aberrant, a departure from what is norm everywhere else. That the salvation provided in the kingdom of God is depicted in terms of the lost being found, the dead being brought back to life again, and the Father's house being filled with the sound of joyous banquet is wholly in accord with the message and conduct of Jesus.[56]

"Revelation is a book not about vindictiveness," Ben Witherington reminds us, "but about vindication, not about the glee of the few over the damnation of the many but about the great cloud of witnesses there will be one day from every tribe, tongue, and nation." [57] "'The two-edged sword' of the Word of God (Rev 19:13) is threatening, but it is also a metaphorical image," argues Christopher C. Rowland, "an effective word, but still *only* a word and not a violent action" (Italics mine).[58] God does render judgment, but it is always linked with divine mercy and is heralded with a summons or warning for readiness or repentance. At the Trinity Institute in New York City, Rossing stated that the central message of the Book of Revelation is that God wants to heal the earth not destroy it. All of the unthinkable plagues and other disasters were to exhort the believers to faithfulness, not a desire on God's part to destroy the earth.[59]

---

56. Beasley-Murray, *Jesus and the Kingdom of God*, 114.
57. Witherington, *Revelation*, 206.
58. Rowland, "The Book of Revelation," *The New Interpreter's Bible*, 701.
59. Rossing, "God's Unfinished Future: Why It Matters Now," The 37th Annual Trinity Institute, Trinity Church, Wall Street, New York, City, January 23, 2007. See also Rossing *The Rapture Exposed*, 84ff.

## CHRISTIAN LIVING

The style of living of the Christians represented in the *Left Behind* novels is at a great distance from the believers to whom the Book of Revelation was first addressed. Like so many other beliefs, this end times fiction has stood the ancient world on its head with its depiction of the modern day Christians and their struggle with the enemies of the world government. Rather than being subservient and martyrs for their faith (though Chloe, Tsion, Buck and some others eventually do die), they live with all the advantages of modern technology. Rather than rejecting technology as linked with the powers of evil, the Tribulation Force uses the best computers, cellular phones, advance weapons like the Uzi, air planes and helicopters, cars like the Land Rover and many other kinds of the latest technology. Often they exhibit superior resources than do the Antichrist forces. This would certainly be the opposite of what it was probably like for the first century Christians. I am not implying that Christians should not utilize the best resources they have at their disposal, especially in sharing the Good News with others and in living a comfortable life. But the heroes in the *Left Behind* novels, however, are depicted as being able to move in economic and other circles that few ordinary Christians would ever have an opportunity to draw upon.

Rayford Steele, Buck Williams and other heroes in the novels are not projected as persons from the lower class of society but are pictured as being from among the elite. Both Rayford and Buck are persons who are well educated and have reached the top of their particular vocational fields and have wealth and prestige. They freely use their wide knowledge, influential friends, contacts, resources, skills and wealth to accomplish their goals and get the equipment and other necessities to withstand the evils of the satanic forces. They do not hesitate to use all of the material resources they can find for the work of the Tribulation Force. When Rayford takes Chloe, Buck and Hattie to an expensive restaurant with the unannounced agenda of talking to them about his religious experience, he uses his financial resources to give him privacy with them. He turns to the waiter and states:

> "We'd like to spend another hour or so here if it is all right." "Sir, we do have an extensive reservation list—"I wouldn't want this table to be less than profitable for you," Rayford said, pressing a large bill into the waiter's palm, "so boot us out whenever it becomes neces-

sary." The waiter peeked at the bill and slipped it into his pocket. "I'm sure you will not be disturbed," he said. And the water glasses were always full.[60]

This is just a small indication of the modern, worldly kinds of persons that compose the *Left Behind* characters. Buck's decision to buy a Range Rover, the most powerful car he can find under six figures regardless of what it might do to the environment reflects not only his financial resources but his lack of concern for the pollution of the air or what may happen to the earth. If there are only seven years before the end, what does it matter? "The novels graphic fixation on plagues, war, rapture and end-times violence," Barbara Rossing observes in an interview with the editor of The Christian Century, "can too easily lead to the escapist idea that we could trash this planet."[61] The characters in the novels remind me of the sophisticated and suave James Bond with all his fancy gadgets and the financial and technological resources they had on the "Mission Impossible" team, smart and very resourceful. This may make for interesting fiction but it is far removed from where the first century believers were or where most Christians are today. A disregard for the world we live in and its environment and a limitless consumer mentality are not healthy models for Christians living today. The theological interpretation that suggests that a time is coming for Christians that they should be unconcerned about caring for the earth and its resources is a frightening teaching.

## OTHER RELIGIOUS GROUPS

In the *Left Behind* novels a one-world religion is created by Carpathia to establish what he calls "a new era of tolerance and unity." This new religion was called Enigma Babylon One World Faith. All world religions and faiths were lumped together as one basic, worldwide religion. Peter Matthews doesn't believe that the Bible is inspired any more than other religious writings, nor that Jesus was born of a virgin, or rose from the dead, or that Christianity is the only true path to salvation. The new Pontifex Maximus Peter issued the following official Enigma Babylon declaration:

---

60. LaHaye and Jenkins, *Left Behind*, 382.

61. "End Game: Living Joyfully in an Apocalyptic Time," an interview with Barbara Rossing in *The Christian Century* (November 14, 2006).

> *To say arbitrarily . . . that the Jewish and Protestant Bible, containing the Old and New Testaments, is the final authority for faith and practice, represents the height of intolerance and disunity. It flies in the face of all we have accomplished, and adherents to that false doctrine are hereby considered heretics.*[62] *(Italics his)*

This folding of all religions into one is LaHaye's way of expressing clandestine-like his disapproval of the National and World Council of Churches. LaHaye states that although Pontifex Matthews may appear to be a work of fiction, he cites Episcopal bishop, John Spong, as an example of this figure today. He sees "the deadening effects of apostasy" in the teachings of the National and World Council of Churches, the decline in church attendance in the Methodist and Presbyterian churches, the apostate teaching in seminaries like Union Theological Seminary in New York City, and in other seminaries and mainline churches.[63] Most churches other than fundamental churches like Good Hope Village mentioned in the prequel, *The Regime*, and in the other novels are depicted not only as not preaching the authentic faith but are described as boring, dancing around the truth, offering only inspirational thoughts like "mostly made up stories of long lost kittens finding their way home".[64]

Most Roman Catholics find the *Left Behind* novels very anti-Catholic. The novels clearly to identify that the Catholic Church, with its seat of power in Rome, has become, through former Pope Matthews, the new leader of the apostate one-world religion. The figure and style of behavior and leadership are ridiculed through the novels. In several of his nonfiction books, like *Are We Living in the End Times?*, *Rapture Under Attack* and *Revelation Unveiled*, LaHaye condemns the Catholic Church as apostate. He calls Catholicism "Babylonian mysticism" and an "idolatrous religion." He states that "between A.D. 607 to today, the Universal (Catholic) Church headquartered in Rome gradually became more Babylonian than Christian."[65] In the novels the center of religion is moved from Rome to Babylon to symbolize the idolatrous nature of the Church. In his commentary LaHaye attacks Catholicism by showing what he calls its "similarity to paganism." This theme is made in subdued ways

---

62. LaHaye and Jenkins, *Tribulation Force*, 401.
63. LaHaye and Jenkins, *Are We Living in the End Times?*, 67–68, 76–78.
64. LaHaye and Jenkins, *The Regime*, 203, 259.
65. LaHaye, *Revelation Unveiled*, 67.

but evident to those familiar with his other writings. Catholic scholars like Carl E. Olson and a number of Catholic bishops have strongly condemned the *Left Behind* series as anti-Catholic in content and form.[66]

LaHaye and other dispensationalists view the founding of Israel in 1948 as a nation once again as a clear prophetic sign that the Rapture is near. Israel must have its original borders restored. And then one event must happen, according to LaHaye before the Rapture can occur, and that is that the temple must be rebuilt on its old site in Jerusalem.[67] This concept is based on their strange interpretation of Daniel 9:26–27. The site of the old temple of Israel is the Dome of the Rock, the third holiest site for Muslims, where it has been since A.D. 691 Many fundamentalists are trying to find ways to get the site restored to Israel so the Jewish temple can be rebuilt on that location. This continues to be a very volatile issue in Middle East politics. In the *Left Behind* novels the Muslims agree graciously to have the Dome of the rock moved to "New Babylon" in Iraq so the Jews can rebuild the temple. Imagine what would happen in the tense Middle East if such a proposal were ever suggested today.

The *Left Behind* series with all its emphasis on Israel and the rebuilding of the temple is still strongly anti-Semitic. The picture of the Jews represents a stubborn people who have continued to deny that Jesus is the Messiah. The Jewish heroes are converts from Judaism to Christianity like Tsion Ben-Judah, a former rabbinical scholar and an Israeli statesman who preaches to a billion persons daily and later to the Jews in Petra and in Jerusalem and Dr. Chaim Rosenzweig, Noble Prize winning Israeli botanist and statesman who murders Carpathia. During the last days before the "Glorious Appearing", thousands of Jews are converted by the preaching of Tsion and they accept Jesus as the Messiah. The Jews who did not accept Christ suffered the awful "judgments" of God during the tribulation and were beheaded by the Antichrist forces for not having the "mark". They received punishment both from God and Satan.

One of the dramatic moments in the novels is when Tsion announced unexpectedly on a special CNN television report that went out to millions of viewers many of whom were Jewish, that he had been converted to Christianity.

---

66. See Olson, *Will Catholics Be Left Behind?*, 56–65; www.crisismagazine.com/november2003/olson.htm; www.sldmfishers.org/Left%20Behind%20-Bad%20Theology%20and%20Anti-Catholic.

67. LaHaye and Jenkins, *Are We Living in the End Times?*, 127–29.

"Jesus Christ is the Messiah!" The rabbi concluded. "There can be no other option. I had come to this answer but was afraid to act on it, and I was almost too late. Jesus came to rapture his church, to take them with him to heaven as he said he would. I was not among them, because I wavered. But I have since received him as my Savior. He is coming back in seven years! Be ready!"[68]

Jews in the *Left Behind* series are some of the main "targets" for conversion to complete the number of the 144,000 believers before the Glorious Appearing.

Not only are other religious bodies like the National and World Council of Churches, Catholicism and Jews portrayed in negative images, but the novels also attack feminism and women's rights, homosexuals and present a strong male chauvinism with the dominance of Americans over other racial groups in the world. LaHaye has enforced his right-wing agenda in various places throughout the series. A healthy, mature attitude toward other religious groups and those who differ with us is absent from these novels. Other significant social and ethical issues are ignored or glossed over. A sound model for Christian living today is not depicted in this series. It is an unrealistic fictional account of life lived in the "meantime" in anticipation of the return of Christ. LaHaye's Rapture theology calls the Christian far a field from where Jesus has instructed us to live as the "light," the "leaven," and the "salt" of the earth.

## CRITICISM AND RIDICULE

The *Left Behind* series has focused so sharply on the wrath of God that it in turn has received the wrath of some of its readers who have become harsh critics. When it projects such a distortion of biblical and theological concepts, it is impossible to remain silent. And I have chosen to address the problem. Some conservative writers have expressed a different sort of anger. Lisa Ruby has written a book entitled, *God's Wrath on Left Behind: Exposing the Antichrist Agenda of the Left Behind Series*. She avows that the *Left Behind* series promotes unhealthy sexual activity, suicide, murder, new age tenets and other problems for the Christian. The gore, violence, blood, directed suffering and twisted concepts of God and Christ loom as a major issue with me about the novels as a Christian tool for instruction. If the later novels in the series are made into movies they will have to be at

---

68. LaHaye and Jenkins, *Tribulation Force*, 396.

least R rated for the violence alone. Why is it that so many people are still attracted to movies or books that focus on violence? Is it the moth being attracted to the flame and experiencing its own demise?

The end times series has not only received the wrath of some writers but it has also been the subject of ridicule and parody by several writers, note in particular *Right Behind: A Parody of Last Days Goofiness* by Nathan D. Wilson and *Kiss My Left Behind* by Earl Lee.[69] More than just humorous, these books critique the fundamentalists who prey on the gullibility of those who want absolute certainty in religion. Wilson observes that the readers who like the *Left Behind* novel may feel "wounded and offended" by parodies or criticism. "But that is," he states, "the tiresome refuge of every little god who thinks blasphemy restrictions apply to him."[70] When someone bases their books on strange, biblical prefabrications, like LaHaye and Jenkins have done, they are open to both criticism and ridicule.

---

69. Wilson, *Right Behind* and Lee, *Kiss My Left Behind*.
70. Wilson, *Right Behind*, 107.

7

## Moving Forward Faithfully

For some readers of the *Left Behind* novels any critiquing of these writings is like criticizing the Bible itself. Unfortunately, they have viewed the *Left Behind* interpretation of the Scriptures as gospel itself. I have tried to help readers see the inadequacies and abuses of their theological and biblical interpretations. The good news, of course, is that there are more competent ways to interpret the Book of Revelation and eschatology than what the *Left Behind* novels purpose. In fact, throughout most of the Church's history this was indeed the case. The dispensationalist's views of Darby, LaHaye, Lindsey and others are rather recent in the history of the Church. As I indicated in the first chapter, the Rapture concept dates from the latter part of the nineteenth century. And most legitimate scholars discredit it today. Christians have been faithful even though the views of dispensationalism were foreign to them.

Our faithful discipleship does not depend on sensationalism and distorted interpretations of Scripture. There are positive possibilities and implications for faithful living that accompany a more orthodox and respectable understanding of the Christian life and end times. Our purpose in examining the *Left Behind* theology was not to dismantle anyone's faith but to help us build our faith on a solid ground of biblical and theological truth.

I want to offer five guidelines to help mark the trail as we seek to follow Christ and build a meaningful faith as we journey along the way toward our final goal. The call to follow Christ is a summons to discipleship and a commitment to endure until the end. It is a journey that is not always easy and is sometimes filled with mountaintops of inspiration and valleys of struggles and sorrows. But it is a journey that is filled with special joy that arises from the companionship of the presence of a living Lord who goes ahead of us on the path to guide the way. We follow knowing that our Lord knows what the end of the trail will be like. So we proceed with confidence and hope.

## 1. ACCEPT THE NEED FOR CONTINUOUS GROWTH

A person begins the journey with Christ through what is called a "new birth" experience. When one gives his or her life to Christ that marks the beginning not the end of one's Christian spiritual experience. A lifetime of potential growth lies before us. Every Christian should ask himself or herself the question: "Have I grown deeper in my faith today than I was a year ago or five years ago? Do I understand the essence of the Christian life, joy and radiance better today than when I first became a Christian?" If not, there is something radically wrong with where I am in my Christian journey. First we become a Christian and then we grow. Being always precedes becoming. We first are, then we become. Once we are, then we have potential of becoming more.

Growth never takes place, I am convinced, except on the edges of our lives where we are exposed to something unknown to us. If we remain only where we have already been, we cannot grow. As some edge of our life is exposed to that which we have not yet experienced, we are exposed to more than we have already begun to be, then we begin to become more than we are. Growth comes as we are stimulated and we move to become more than we are. We cannot become new persons without exposure to the new. We grow through those encounters. When we are satisfied with what we are individually, death begins to take place. The alternative to growth is regression, decay and corruption. If a talent is buried in the soil, as our Lord reminded us, it does not develop. If we cling to our security blankets of only the known, secure and familiar, then the challenges of the new and unexplored will be missed. There is life only where there is growth. If there is no growth, there is no life. Sometimes with growth some pain occurs. Birth is not without pain. Every new idea, insight, discovery and advance may have some pain in its entrance into life. We need to be open so we can be responsive to the God who is calling us to be more than we are.

### *Thinking Is A Religious Duty*

The famous German philosopher, Hegel, expressed his view about the relationship between thinking and religion in these words: "To think and to think hard is a religious duty." To commit your life to Christ is not a call to surrender your mind. William James, the American philosopher, once wrote: "I like tender hearts, but I like tough minds." We need to use our mind. Tough Christian minds are those who are able to bring about what the tenderhearted want. Do not believe those people who will tell you that the Christian faith is linked with sentimental approaches. We have to use our mind and think hard about the great issues of life. The questions of suffering, pain, war, poverty and all the others demand that we use our mind. We have to use our mind with all of its creativity, imagination, power and potential.

Down through the centuries there have been great thinkers who have given their minds as well as their hearts to service to God and truth. Christians like Paul, Athanasius, Augustine, Aquinas, Luther, Calvin, Wesley, Schweitzer and thousands of others, have believed that to love God with all one's mind is not separate from what it means to be a Christian. These persons were not aware that to be a believer was somehow divorced from being a thinker. That is indeed a sacred duty. We are challenged to love God with all our mind. A Christian is not one who will believe anything or respond to every sentimental, sensational or emotional appeal. He or she is committed to loving God with all of one's mind.

In his autobiographical sketch of his theological journey, *Bound and Free: A Theologian's Journey*, Douglas John Hall, Emeritus Professor of Theology at McGill University in Montreal, Quebec, challenges us with the necessity having a "thinking faith." He reminds us that we never have absolute certainty in our spiritual journey. He attests that God offers us an alternative to certitude which is called "trust." We follow in the steps of one of Jesus' disciples, doubting Thomas, whom Hall calls the first Protestant.[1] Our faith journey may often be filled with doubt as well as faith, but we travel with trust, not blind, unquestioning faith. A thinking faith requires us to be open to God, to others and their religious perspectives and to journey with Paul Tillich's "the Protestant principle" in mind, which "implies that there cannot be a sacred system, ecclesiastical or political; that there cannot be a sacred hierarchy with absolute authority; and that there cannot be a truth in human minds which is divine truth in itself."[2] We never know with absolute certainty. Who can ever know God's ways or

---

1. Hall, *Bound and Free*, 99–105.
2. Tillich, *The Protestant Era*, 226.

God's presence so clearly that another perspective or understanding is not possible? We trust and travel with the awareness that faith is always mixed with some doubts. But this awareness keeps us from arrogance and pride. Always strive for a "thinking" faith.

*Resources For Guidance*

Many have turned to the *Left Behind* novels because they wanted to know what is going to happen in the future, and these novels asserted that they are doing that. One of the articles I saw about the end times fiction warned the readers not to leave their brain behind when they read the novels. Approach these novels by being informed by reading some good commentaries and other literature about apocalyptic writings. Some of these sources have been mentioned in the endnotes. Some good commentaries for a lay person are the following: William Barclay, *The Revelation of John*, two volumes (Philadelphia: The Westminster Press, 1960), Julian Price Love, *The Layman's Bible Commentary*, volume 25 (Richmond: John Knox Press, 1960), James L. Blevins, *Revelation* (Atlanta: John Knox Press, 1984). These are older but still helpful resources.

For a more detailed study, I would recommend the following commentaries: M. Eugene Boring, *Revelation* in the Interpretation series (Louisville: John Knox Press, 1989), Kenneth H. Maahs, *Of Angels, Beasts and Plagues* (Valley Forge: Judson Press, 1999), Mitchell G. Reddish, *Revelation*, Smyth & Helwys Bible Commentary (Mercer, GA.: Smyth & Helwys, 2001), Christopher C. Rowland, *The Book of Revelation* in the New Interpreter's Bible, volume XII (Nashville: Abingdon Press, 1998). The only commentary that I know that actually discusses the *Left Behind* series is by Ben Witherington III, *Revelation: The New Cambridge Bible Commentary* (New York: Cambridge, 2003). Dr. Witherington is professor at Asbury Seminary in Kentucky. The best way to find references to the end times fiction in this commentary is to look in the Author Index under LaHaye and the Subject Index under dispensationalism or check the Scripture Index. These books can help the reader understand what kind of book Revelation is and get a more realistic grasp of its real meaning.

I want to encourage you to keep on thinking, studying and growing as a Christian.

### Spiritual Growth Is Never Complete

None of us ever reaches the point where he or she can claim, "I am full grown spiritually." We are continuously challenged to be the full, whole, complete, mature person God has created us to be. Let me encourage you to continue growing and developing. To love God with all of one's mind is to acknowledge that our education is never complete. We are always in the process of becoming. Keep on growing and developing! The only person I know who is the least educated and mature is the individual who says that he or she has arrived educationally. None of us can say, "I'm done with learning." No one ever really is!

In order to grow spiritually or in any way, one has to remain open and responsive to new insights, directions, ideas, thoughts, discoveries, adventures or unknown trails. In the process of becoming, we either go forward or backward. There is no area of neutrality. We are both growing and moving forward so that our mind, heart, and being are progressing or we are regressing, moving backwards. Let continuous spiritual growth be one of the bright markers on your spiritual pathway.

## 2. ATTEST TO THE MYSTERY OF LIFE

As you travel along your spiritual path, I would encourage you to note the marker that attests to the mystery of God and the universe God has created, including human kind. It is so easy to want simple, literal answers to complicated, incomprehensible, obscure or transcendental questions about God, suffering, good, evil and the Scriptures. The *Left Behind* novels often remove the depth of genuine meaning and mystery in the Book of Revelation by interpreting the Apocalypse and other apocalyptic literature literally. But our religion cannot always be displayed in only black and white. There are colors in it that reach beyond our imagination. Paul reminds us that "we see in a mirror dimly" (1Cor. 13:12 NRSV). Often to interpret literally the images and strange figures of the Book of Revelation is to make them preposterous and nonsensical. I want to encourage you to follow the sign marked mystery as you journey along your spiritual trail.

### The Mystery Of God's Presence

I believe that the entire universe is shrouded with the mystery of God's presence. Look around you! Where do you see God? The mystery of God's presence is revealed in a sunrise and sunset, in the flight of a bumblebee, in the chirping of a cricket, in the songs of birds, in the migration of birds, in the house which a wasp builds, in a web which a spider spins, in the green shoot from a newly planted seed, in a butterfly as it emerges from its chrysalis, in a lightening bug, in the flight of a hummingbird, in the roadway of a leaf, in the beating of the human heart, in the circulation of blood within our body, in the conception and birth of a baby, in the ability to think, in the defense system of a skunk, in the sweetness of sugar, in the restlessness of a tornado and in the ceaseless rhythm of ocean waves breaking on the shore.

Look around you and you will see that the mystery of life cannot be understood easily nor defined simply. The older I get the more I am aware of what I can neither understand nor explain about life all around me, within me, above me or below me. There is more that I do not understand than that I can explain. This mystery of life all around me pulls me on a never-ending journey toward discovering the "not yet known" or "the still to be discovered" worlds that lie ahead of me.

Loren Eiseley, the poetic anthropologist, in his book, *The Unexpected Universe*, points to the "mystery" of the universe.

> Some years previously, I had written a little book of essays in which I had narrated how time had become natural in our thinking; I had gone on to speak likewise of life and man. In the end, however, I had been forced to ask, How Natural is Natural?—a subject that raised the hackles of some of my scientifically inclined colleagues who confuse the achievements of their disciplines with the certitude on a cosmic scale. (He notes that his question implied an "ill-concealed heresy" for science.) The word contains for all of its seeming regularity, a series of surprises resembling those that in childhood terrorized us by erupting on springs from closed boxes.[3]

### Whispers About God

The natural universe, even from a scientific viewpoint, is not so easily understood. It is filled with surprises. We live on the edge of mystery. All around us there are gestures, intimations, suggestions, and whispers of the mystery of God's presence. Every sunrise is a whisper of the mystery of God. A newly fallen snow is a whisper of God's presence. Music, especially Christmas music, is a whisper of God's presence. Poetry, art,

---

3. Eiseley, *The Unexpected Universe*, 31.

architecture and literature are all whispers of God's presence. Worship is a whisper of God's presence. Even science is a whisper of God's presence. "God does not die on the day when we cease to believe in a personal deity," Dag Hammarskjold wrote, "but we die on the day when our lives cease to be illumined by a steady radiance, renewed daily, of a wonder, the source of which is beyond all reason."[4]

A sense of mystery, which we see supremely in the Christmas stories and the universe around us, should remove all dogmatism from life. How dare any person assert that he or she has the final handle—understanding—knowledge of—or "complete" theological system about God, especially the end times? The audacity of such a claim is frightening. If God is constantly making God's presence known in varied ways, whispering here and there in so many ways, how can we presume to limit the divine's disclosure or confine God to our neat theological system?

## Beyond Rational Knowledge

Have you heard about a group of East Tennessee folks who claimed that only Baptists had the whole truth about God? And they went another step further, "If there is any one group of Baptists that understand what this whole truth is," they asserted, "it is this East Tennessee Baptist Church which understands it better than anybody else."

The sheer audacity of such a claim is staggering to the mind. How can any person believe that she or he has totally grasped the mysteries about God? Our mind cannot begin to contain but a vague description of the edge of God's "garments." God's ways are always beyond our perceptions, aspirations and even hopes. Our intellect cannot fully grasp all that God is, was, and will be. God's being and ways are beyond logic and argument. God often blows our theological and philosophical systems apart, because God is constantly surprising us by revealing the divine presence in ways and places differently from what we had expected.

If light passes through a prism, that light is refracted and comes out as red on one end of the spectrum and violet on the other end. These and the colors between are the colors that can be seen with the human eye. But . . . But with special instruments other colors are present, but the human eye is not able to perceive them. Isn't this even truer about God? There is a mystery about God's presence that goes beyond anything we can begin to

---

4. Hammarskjöld, *Markings*, 56.

understand. What would our forefathers and mothers of a hundred years ago think about television, sputniks or computers in our present world? They would have thought such things impossible. We live on the edge of mystery all of life. And we cannot expect to understand totally by peering through a telescope, microscope or through our small intellect. God is constantly being revealed in unexpected places and ways.

This awareness calls us to remain open to and teachable by God wherever and however God chooses. In the day of Jesus, most of the religious leaders missed his coming because they had limited and restricted how a person could know God and the divine ways. Are we not in constant danger of doing the same thing today? As the common expression reminds us, "The shoe must not tell the foot how big to get." We as God's children, like fertile soil, should lie open and responsive to the sacred coming, whatever way God chooses.

### *The Presence At The Communion Table*

Every time we gather at the Communion Table, we attest to the mystery of the living presence of our Lord. The Bread and Cup point us to the continuous mystery of his abiding presence among us. We gather at the Communion Table not to reflect on the memory of a dead teacher from the ancient past, but to open our awareness to the Presence of a living Lord who meets us at this Table. The elements of bread and wine call us to reflect on the mystery of sacrificial love and undeserved grace.

Every time I perform or witness a baptismal service, I affirm again the mystery of God's redemption and grace and conversion and discipleship. The water of baptism provokes the mystery of redemption and transformation. Every step of the Christian's walk reminds me of the non-rational factor of the "Numinous Other" and "Mysterium Tremendum" of which Rudolf Otto wrote about over eighty years ago.[5] In the kind of universe in which we live, I choose to follow the mystery marker. I encourage you to do the same.

### 3. AFFIRM THE GREAT DOCTRINES OF THE CHURCH

One of the essential markers along our trail is the centrality of our Christian beliefs. For centuries Christians have been guided through life by the assurance of these beliefs. To exchange a fabricated concept like

---

5. Otto, *The Idea of the Holy*.

Rapture, which is proposed in the *Left Behind* novels, is to jettison the foundational stone of our Christian belief. To speak of two returns of Jesus is to deny the clear teachings of the Church through the centuries and the New Testament itself.

## *Expressions Of Our Faith*

Christians from all walks of Christendom have affirmed our essential beliefs in such community statements as *The Apostles' Creed*, dating to about A.D. 340, *The Nicene Creed*, (325 A.D.), *The Westminster Confession of Faith*, (1643), Baptist Confessions of Faith like *The First Confession* (1646), *The Second Confession* (1677), *The Philadelphia Confession* (1742), *The Hampshire Confession* (1833), *The Baptist Faith and Message* (1925, 1963, 2000), and the Quakers' "The Chief Principles of the Christian Religion" (1678).[6] The historic doctrines need to be studied and an appreciation for the rich meaning of creation, redemption, atonement, resurrection and other central beliefs need to be affirmed. Christians may never affirm only one interpretation of any of these cardinal beliefs but to disregard any of them for some fictional doctrine is difficult to comprehend.

## *The Centrality Of The Resurrection*

I would caution the reader to consider the grave danger in exchanging the belief in the resurrection for the concept of the Rapture. The loss to our faith would be unrecoverable. The resurrection was at the center of the early church's teachings. When Jesus proclaimed, "I am the resurrection" (John 11:25), we acknowledged that this is why we celebrate Easter today. Jesus Christ offers the radical difference in the newness of real life. The resurrection life he offers can be in no other.

To note the difference the resurrection made in the life of the first Christians, all one has to do is to observe the defeat and fear of the disciples after the crucifixion as they gathered in the Upper Room. They were frightened that they, too, might be put to death like their Lord. They were dejected and in despair. The One that they had hoped was the promised Messiah had been crucified. They were ashamed because they had fled and not stayed with him during his ordeal on the cross. All of their

---

6. For example, Bettenson, *Documents of the Christian Church*, 34–37, 347–59; Lumpkin, *Baptist Confessions of Faith* and *The Baptist Faith and Message*, both can be found on the Southern Baptist Convention Web site.

hopes, all of their dreams, all that they longed for, they felt were gone. So they gathered in that small room, feeling only despair and hopelessness. Bur when the risen Lord appeared, they were radically transformed. The resurrection of Jesus Christ is the foundation of the Church. It was what made all of the difference in the lives of the disciples indeed. It filled their preaching and writings as they affirmed the One who proclaimed: "I am the resurrection."

*References To The Resurrection*

Note some of the passages in the New Testament which affirm the importance of the resurrection" "With great power the apostles gave their witnesses of the resurrection of the Lord Jesus; and great grace was upon them all" (Acts 17:33). "Paul preached Jesus and the resurrection" (Acts 17:8). "At Athens when they heard of the resurrection of the dead, some mocked" (Acts 17:32). "Before Felix Paul preached the resurrection both of the just and the unjust" (Acts 24:15). Then writing to the Corinthian church, Paul said, "If Christ has not been raised, then our preaching is in vain. Your faith is also in vain . . . You are still in your sins. If in this life only we have hope in Christ, we of all persons are most pitiful but now has Christ been raised from the dead." (1 Cor. 15:14–20).

In another epistle Paul wrote to the Ephesians, "That you may know the exceeding greatness of his power to us who believe according to the working strength of his might which he wrought in Christ, when he raised him from the dead, and made him to sit at the right hand of the heavenly Father" (Eph. 1:18–21). To the Philippians, "That I might know the power of his resurrection" (Phlm. 3:10). In Hebrews, "He ever lives to make intercession for us" (Heb. 7:25). In 1Pet.: "Blessed be the God and Father of our Lord Jesus Christ, who according to his great mercy begat us again unto a living hope by the resurrection of Jesus Christ from the dead" (1 Peter 1:3). Then in Revelation: "Behold, cries the risen Christ, I am alive for evermore and I have the keys of death and Hades" (Rev 1:18).

*The Foundation Stone Of Our Faith*

There is no question that the resurrection is the foundation stone of our faith. I will not exchange it for anything else. Without the resurrection, the cross would have stood for the death of a good teacher, not a redeeming Lord. Without the resurrection, there would be no atonement, no

Church, no sacraments, no Second Coming, no New Testament, no hope of eternal life. All of our beliefs rest on this foundational stone. If it is removed, nothing remains. Eduard Schweizer begins his article in *A New Handbook of Christian Theology* with the affirmation that "resurrection was the heart of the early preaching of Paul, and it has been formative for Christian faith ever since."[7] Writing about Paul's vigorous defense of the resurrection of Christ, Dale Moody observes, "His resurrection is preliminary to any clear prospects for our resurrection, and the validity of the gospel is threatened by a denial of the resurrection of Christ."[8]

When I was pastor at St Matthews Baptist Church in Louisville, Kentucky, Wayne Oates, the noted pastoral counselor and professor, preached one Sunday and made a reference to a trip Sir William Osler, a pioneer physician in medicine, made to Europe from the United States. The ship he was on was accidentally hit by another ship that pierced a hole in the side of the ship. Everyone on board was filled with anxiety. "We have the situation in hand," the crew claimed. "It is under control." He discovered later that the way they had everything under control was in the way the ship itself was built. It had been constructed so that if it received any kind of damage, watertight sealed doors could be closed around the one hole. They could carry a certain amount of water and still get to port safely for repairs.[9]

The resurrection of Christ gives me that kind of assurance. The New Testament witness to his resurrection comforts me when I think about my own death and the death of my loved ones and others I know. "Everything is under control" because Christ lives. I will continue to follow that marker because it illumines the dark path that stretches past the end. With a risen Lord, I, all of us, can face the end with confidence whenever and however it comes, because he lives, we shall live also.

## 4. ACKNOWLEDGE THE NEED FOR FAITHFULNESS

One of the major teachings of the Book of Revelation is John's resounding call for fidelity among the Christians as they faced persecution and suffering. But Christian persecution is not unknown in our own days. As I was writing this chapter I read about the arrest of one-hundred house church

---

7. Schweizer, "Revelation," 402.
8. Moody, *The Word of Truth*, 505.
9. Oates, "The Daily Providence of God."

Christians in the westernmost region of China, Xinjiang Autonomous Region and fines and pressure that were directed on unregistered Baptists in Astana Kazakhstan as well as police raiding a service of worship.[10] These are remote parts of the earth to us, nevertheless, they are a reminder that persecution of Christians can still happen today.

### More Subtle Persecutions

For most of us, however, we will likely never face that kind of overt persecution. Christians today are confronted with more subtle tests to our faithfulness. Our struggles may take the form of being ignored or snubbed by others because of our Christian commitment. We may not be invited to share in certain groups, organizations or inner circles. We may at times suffer ridicule or misunderstanding. We may be considered odd because we still believe that attending church for worship and Bible study are important or we do not want to engage in some form of office, school or "free time" activities. To stand tall for honesty, integrity, justice, morality, compassion and other Christian values will not always be easy. The Christian is engaged in a continuous battle with the forces of evil.

### The Reality Of Evil

As Christians we have to acknowledge the presence and power of the forces of evil in the world. The Christians and Church are always under attack from the powers of evil. The Christian life is a constant warfare against evil. In his day, the apostle Paul saw these forces of evil as demonic and spiritual in nature. Today we are likely to sense the demonic power deep within ourselves and in the corrupt forces of society.

We do acknowledge that evil is real! We see the power of evil in the life of a teenager caught under the hypnotic stare of drugs. Its evidence is visible in the college student who is shot and paralyzed for life. Its power is seen in the continuous piling of nuclear weapons, the threats of terrorists, the Arab-Israeli struggle, the corruption in business and politics, the unwillingness to confront the environmental and global warming crisis, and in the sexual distortions on TV, in the movies and in many magazines. We can also look into the dark abyss of our own souls and we recognize the power of evil. We know our own selfishness, envy, jealousy, vindictiveness, lust, sexual passions and lying. There is darkness within us as well as around us.

---

10. *The Western Recorder*, Louisville, Kentucky (August 17, 2004), 10.

## The Call To Faithfulness

Acknowledging the reality of evil, the Christian, nevertheless, is charged to remain faithful to Christ during this struggle. Some have experienced rejection, suffering and pain in following Christ and have turned away for a more comfortable life. They desired a more comfortable or convenient life-style. If following Christ is going to be filled with difficulties and problems, they prefer a way that seems more reasonable and less demanding. So they dropped away from Christ and his Church. Sometimes the allure of the world pulls us away from Christ and we give in to its enticement and charms.

Each of us must make choices in our relationship to Jesus Christ. We make choices daily. Either we choose to forsake Christ for the world or we forsake the world for Christ. The apostle Paul chose to continue following Christ who had appeared to him and to whom he had given his life. In following Christ, it became demanding and difficult and he ended up in prison and finally was put to death. But he was willing to keep on keeping on.

## Finishing The Journey

God calls us not only to start the journey but also to finish it. We not only find a place of beginning in our race, but we are to continue until the end. We have all seen an athlete start off with a great beginning but can't keep up his or her pace and soon fades away. We have seen the student who starts off the semester saying, "Boy, I'm really going to study this year." And within a few weeks he or she has fallen into the same old pattern that too often has been taken. Goals, dreams and visions of what Christ wants us to be are essential to lead us beyond where we presently are in our Christian journey. Sometimes our aspirations may not become reality. For some of us, however, we may stumble through life because our assurance of Christ's presence is not real enough. He is ever present, but for some reason we do not sense it. As we open our spirit to him, we can follow and be strengthened in our time of weakness.

We are challenged to continue the race of life until it is completed and to remain faithful to the One who has set our feet on the spiritual path. The church cannot expect to change the world without the faithfulness of its believers in the time of suffering or personal trials. Jesus said, "The one who endures to the end will be saved" (Mark 13:13). The bright marker of faithfulness is essential to complete the journey through life, especially during the times of temptation, suffering, distress, anxiety, torment, etc. We can take comfort and reassurance from the words of Jesus in the Book of Revelation: "Be faithful until death, and I will give you the crown of life" (Rev 2:10).

### 5. APPROACH THE FUTURE WITH CONFIDENCE

Books like the *Left Behind* novels might provoke fear and uncertainty about the future and raise what seem like unanswerable questions about the end or suggest unrealistic claims about one's knowledge about the end times. As a Christian, one should face the future with confidence in God's love and providence, but this does not give any grounds for arrogance and self-righteousness. Humility should always be the stance of a believer and not dogmatism as we advance along the path of life toward that mysterious lodging which Christ has gone before us to prepare for us.

No one can ever put on God's "glasses" and expect to know absolutely what is going to happen in the end times. The Scriptures do assure us that God will be sovereign and God's reign will bring new beginnings and new creations with justice and righteousness for all persons. As Christians, we do not have to have some visible sign on our forehead to reassure us that we have committed our lives to Christ. We walk by faith and the assurance of the presence of a living Lord. We travel by faith not by sight.

*Anticipation*

When you find the marker of confidence, I believe you can face the future with anticipation. There is no crystal ball, fortuneteller, Ouija board or horoscope or dispensationalist's preacher who can give us a guarantee about tomorrow. As we travel, we search and pray to sense God's direction and will along the path. When I have searched for God's guidance, I have often sensed an inner response that said, "Walk in the light you already have. Follow the knowledge that you understand in the present moment. Walk in that light." If we are walking on a dark night, we can use a flashlight to help us see the path before us. We can shine a beam of light a short distance in front of us and then walk in that light. As we walk in the lighted path immediately in front of us, we can walk further along the path. As you move into the future, walk in the light that you see in front of you. You will never be able to see all the way to the end of your path.

Walk in whatever light you have. As you follow in that light, God will give you more light and insight along the path. I hope you will seek to follow the light that God will provide for you.

## A Positive Spirit

Although we can never fully know nor predict with accuracy what the future will be like, we do not have to submit to pessimism or despair. George Bernard Shaw once wrote: "Do you know what a pessimist is? A pessimist is a man (or a woman) who thinks everybody else is as nasty as himself (or herself) and hates them for it." I don't think that we have to adapt that attitude. As Christians, we need to learn to be positive. Our day is a time for optimism, enthusiasm and affirmation. Don't view life through the pessimistic and dismal "glasses" of the end times prophets who see the world as only getting worse and worse until Jesus comes and takes the believers out of this gloomy world. God has not deserted the world nor does God despise it. God loves the world and all human kind and is seeking to guide us to live in the universe productively and relate more meaningfully and lovingly to each other. Approach the future with hope and excitement.

## The Abiding Presence

The "Seer" in the Book of Revelation was offering hope to believers during a horrible time of persecution and suffering. He did not despair. He trusted in the abiding and sovereign power of the Lamb of God. Our times are nothing compared to those first century struggles, but we still have those words of confidence and hope from the same Christ who goes before us on the trail. Frank Tupper, a professor of theology, who has passed through his own personal valley of grief with the death of his wife, is still bold to assert:

> Jesus trusted his hope to God, and God established our hope in Jesus. God reached through death and beyond it with the gift of eternal life: God raised the crucified Jesus from the dead. He is risen. And what God has done in Jesus, God intends to do for all of us. The song of resurrection concludes the Biblical Story with "Alleluia," an ending already transcended in a new beginning. We live into that new beginning that lies beyond this side of the ending. In the hope of Jesus we trust the God of love.[11]

11. Tupper, *A Scandalous Presence*, 438–39.

The five guidelines I have suggested in this chapter can help place markers along our trail as we follow the living Christ who goes before us. Remember, Jesus is not a dead memory that confines him to the past. Nor is he off in some remote heaven waiting to come back to snatch his followers off the earth. That would mean he has deserted us. No, Christ is present with us now as the risen Savior. "And remember," Jesus told his disciples as he commissioned them to share the gospel with others. "I am with you always to the end of the age" (Matt 28: 20 NRSV).

In the small book, *Echoes of Eternity: Listening to the Father*, Hal M. Helms invites us to pray and hear God speaking to us. He reflects on this last Scripture verse.

> I go before you, My child, and prepare the way. When you walk in My way, your life fulfills My purpose for you. When you follow your own path, the results are dead and lifeless. Redeem the time, My child. These days have been given for purposes you cannot fully see nor understand. Yours is not to view the distant scene, but to stay close to Me and let My will prevail. That is a reward enough for now, and there is much to do.[12]

---

12. Helms, *Echoes of Eternity*, 178–79.

# Bibliography

Abanes, Richard. *End-Time Visions: The Doomsday Obsession*. Bloomington, MN: Bethany House, 1998.
Aune, David E. *Word Bible Commentary: Revelation 6–16*, vol. 52B. Nashville: Thomas Nelson, 1998.
Bakker, Jim. *Prosperity and the Coming Apocalypse*. Nashville: Thomas Nelson, 1998.
Barclay, William. *The Revelation of John*, vol. 1. Philadelphia: Westminster, 1960.
Barr, James. *Fundamentalism*. London: SCM, 1977.
Bauckham, Richard. *The Theology of the Book of Revelation*. Cambridge: Cambridge University Press, 1993.
Beasley-Murray, G. R. *Jesus and the Kingdom of God*. Grand Rapids: Eerdmans, 1986.
———. *The Book of Revelation, The New Century Bible Commentary*. London: Marshall, Morgan & Scott, 1981.
Bettenson, Henry. Editor. *Documents of the Christian Church*. New York: Oxford University Press, 1956.
Birch, Charles and John B. Cobb, Jr., *The Liberation of Life from the Cell to Community*. Cambridge: Cambridge University Press, 1990.
Blevins, James L. "Book of Revelation." In *Mercer Dictionary of the Bible*, edited by Watson E. Mills. Macon, GA: Mercer University Press, 1990.
———. *Revelation As Drama*. Nashville: Broadman, 1986.
Blount, Brian K. *Can I Get a Witness? Reading Revelation through African American Culture*. Louisville: Westminster John Knox, 2005.
———. *Revelation: A Commentary*. Louisville: Westminster John Knox, 2009.
———. "Wreaking Weakness: A Cultural Studies Reading of the Lamb in the Apocalypse," *The Princeton Seminary Bulletin*, ( vol. XXV, no. 3, New Series, 2004), 296.
Boesak, Allan A. *Comfort and Protest: The Apocalypse from a South African Perspective*. Philadelphia: Westminster, 1986.
Boring, M. Eugene. *Revelation: Interpretation, A Bible Commentary for Teaching and Preaching*. Louisville: John Knox, 1989.
Brown, Lester R. *Plan B 2: Rescuing a Planet Under Stress and a Civilization in Trouble*. New York: Norton, 2003.
Bullard, Robert D., editor. *The Quest for Environmental Justice: Human Rights and the Politics of Pollution*. San Francisco: Sierra Club, 2005.
———, editor. *Unequal Protection: Environmental Justice and the Communities of Color*. San Francisco: Sierra Club, 1994.
Burdick, Alan. *Out of Eden: An Odyssey of Ecological Invasion*. New York: Farrar, Straus and Giroux, 2005.
Caird, G. B. *The Revelation of St. John the Divine*. New York: Harper & Row, 1966.

Campolo, Tony. *How to Rescue the Earth Without Worshiping Nature*. Nashville: Thomas Nelson, 1992.

Carson, Rachel. *Silent Spring*. The Fortieth Anniversary Edition. Boston: Houghton, Mifflin, 2002.

Carter, Jimmy. *Our Endangered Values: America's Moral Crisis*. New York: Simon & Schuster, 2005.

Charles, R. H. *A Critical and Exegetical Commentary on the Revelation of St. John*, Vol. 1. Edinburgh: T&T Clark, 1950.

Chesterton, G. K. *Orthodoxy*. New York: Doubleday, 1959.

Cobb, Jr. John B. *Is It Too Late? A Theology of Ecology*. Denton, TX: Environmental Ethics, 1995.

Collins, Adela Yarboro. *Crisis & Catharsis: The Power of the Apocalypse*. Philadelphia: Westminster, 1984.

———. *The Combat Myth in the Book of Revelation*. New York: Scholars, 2001.

Collins, John J. *The Apocalyptic Imagination: An Introduction to Jewish Apocalyptic Literature*, second edition. Grand Rapids: Eerdmans, 1998.

Copeland, Sebatian, et al. *Antarctica: The Global Warning*. New York: Mandale, 2008.

Couch, Mal. "AntiChrist," "Dispensationalism," In *Dictionary of Premillennial Theology: A Practical Guide to the People, Viewpoints, and History of Prophetic Studies*. Grand Rapids, MI: Kregel, 1996.

Darby, J. N. *The Hopes of the Church of God, In Connection with the Destiny of Jesus and the Nations*. London: G. Morris, 1846.

Davis, Devra. *When Smoke Ran Like Water: Tales of Environmental Deception and the Battle Against Pollution*. New York: Basic Books, 2003.

DeMar, Gary. *End Times Fiction*. Nashville: Thomas Nelson, 2001.

Dyer, Charles H., editor. *Bible Prophecy and the Current Middle East Crisis*. Wheaton, IL: Tyndale House. 1991.

———. *The Rise of Babylon: Sign of the End Times*. Chicago: Moody, 2001.

Easterbrook, Gregg. "Finally Feeling the Heat of Global Warming," Commentary, *The Virginia Pilot*, June 25, 2006, 12.

Edwards, Denis. *Jesus and the Cosmos*. New York: Paulist, 2004.

Ehrlich, Paul R. *The Population Bomb*. New York: Ballatine, 1971.

Eiseley, Loren. *The Unexpected Universe*. New York: Harcourt, Brace & World, 1969.

Elder, Frederick. *Crisis in Eden*. Nashville: Abingdon, 1970.

Ellul, Jacque, *Apocalypse: The Book of Revelation*. Translated by George W. Schreiner. New York: Seabury, 1977.

"End Game: Living Joyfully in an Apocalyptic Time," an interview with Barbara Rossing in *The Christian Century*. November 14, 2006.

Evans, Michael D. *Beyond Iraq: The Next Move—Ancient Prophecy and Modern Day Conspiracy Collide*. New York: Warner Faith, 2003.

"Falwell creates new 'values' coalition," Associated Baptist, *Religious Herald*, November 18, 2004, 3

Fiorenza, Elisabeth Schussler. "Toward a Feminist Biblical Hermeneutics: Biblical Interpretation and Liberation Theology." In *The Challenge of Liberation Theology*, edited by Brian Mahan and LaDale Richesin. New York: Orbis, 1981.

———. *Revelation: Vision of a Just World*. Minneapolis: Fortress, 1993.

Ford, J. Massyngberde. *Revelation: The Anchor Bible*. Garden City, NJ: Doubleday, 1975.

Fowler, Jonathan. "Plundered Planet." *Richmond Times Dispatch*. October 22, 2004.

Frykholm, Amy Johnson. *Rapture Culture: Left Behind in Evangelical America.* Oxford: University Press, 2004.
Golden, William. *The Spire.* New York: Harcourt, Brace & World, 1964.
Gore, Al. *An Inconvenient Truth: The Planetary Emergency of Global Warming and What We Can Do About It.* Emmaus, Pa: Rodale, 2006.
———. *Earth in the Balance.* Boston: Houghton Mifflin, 1992.
Graham, Billy. *Approaching Hoofbeats: The Four Horsemen of the Apocalypse.* Waco, Texas: Word, 1983.
Hagee, John C. *Beginning of the End.* Nashville: Thomas Nelson, 1996.
———. *Day of Deception.* Nashville: Thomas Nelson, 1997.
———. *Final Dawn Over Jerusalem.* Nashville: Thomas Nelson, 1999.
Hall, Douglas John. *Bound and Free: A Theologian's Journey.* Minneapolis: Fortress, 2005.
Hammarskjöld, Dag. *Markings.* New York: Alfred A. Knopf, 1964.
Hargrove, Eugene C., editor. *Beyond Spaceship Earth & Environmental Ethics and the Social System.* San Francisco: Sierra Club, 1986.
———. *Foundations of Environmental Ethics.* New York: Prentice Hall, 1989.
Harrison, Paul and Fred Pearce. *AAAS Atlas of Population and Environment.* Berkeley: University Press of California, 2000.
Helms, Hal M. *Echoes of Eternity: Listening to the Father.* Brewster, MA: Paraclete, 1996.
Hitchcock, Mark. *Seven Signs of the End Times.* Sisters Oregon: Multnomah, 2002.
———, and Thomas Ice. *The Truth Behind Left Behind: A Biblical View of the End Times.* Sisters, Oregon: Multnomah, 2004.
Holmes, Cecile S. "Final Book," (Religious News Service) In the *Religious Herald* (April 29, 2004), 4.
Hotz, Robert Lee. "Science on the Front Lines: Researchers Witness Climate Change from Leading Edge," *The Virginia Pilot,* June 25, 2006, A15, 17.
Houghton, John T. *Global Warming: The Complete Briefing.* Cambridge: Cambridge University Press, 2004.
Hull, William E. "Left Behind." In *Christian Ethics Today,* August 2001, vol. 7, No. 4, 5.
———. *John, The Broadman Bible Commentary,* vol. 9. Nashville: Broadman, 1970.
Hunter, George G. *Radical Outreach: The Recovery of Apostolic Ministry & Evangelism.* Nashville: Abingdon, 2003.
Hyatt, Michael S. *The Millennium Bug: The Computer Crisis Is Coming and the Nerds Can't Save You.* Nashville: Thomas Nelson, 1998.
Ice, Thomas and Timothy Demy, editors. *When the Trumpet Sounds.* Eugene, Oregon: Harvest House, 1995.
Jeremiah, David and Carole C. Carlson. *Escape the Night.* Nashville: Word Publishing, 2001.
Joyner, Rick. *The Final Quest for the Torch and the Sword.* Charlotte: MorningStar, 1996.
Keener, Craig. *Revelation: The NIV Application Commentary.* Grand Rapids: Zondervan, 2000.
Kerry, John and Teresa Heinz Kerry. *This Moment on Earth.* New York: Public Affairs, 2007.
Killinger, John. *God, the Devil and Harry Potter.* New York: St. Martin's Press, 2002.
———. *If Christians Were Really Christians.* St. Louis: Chalice, 2009.
———. *The Life, Death and Resurrection of Harry Potter.* Macon, GA: Mercer University Press, 2009.

Knupp, Fred and Miriam Horn. *Earth: The Sequel: The Race to Reinvent Energy and Stop Global Warming.* New York: W. W. Norton & Company, 2008.

Kraus, C. Norman. *Dispensationalism in America: Its Rise and Development.* Richmond, VA: John Knox, 1958.

Lacayo, Richard. "The Lure of the Cult?" *Time.* April 7, 1997. 45.

LaHaye, Tim. *Prophecy Study Bible.* Nashville: Thomas Nelson, 2001.

———. *Revelation Unveiled.* Grand Rapids: Zondervan, 1999.

———. *The Beginning of the End.* Wheaton, IL: Tyndale House, 1972.

———. *The Rapture Who Will Face the Tribulation?* Eugene, Oregon: Harvest House, 2002.

———. *Understanding Bible Prophecy For Yourself* . Eugene, Oregon: Harvest House, 2001.

LaHaye, Tim and Jerry Jenkins. *Apollyon: The Destroyer Is Unleashed.* Wheaton, IL: Tyndale House, 1999.

———. *Are We Living in the End Times?* Wheaton, IL: Tyndale House, 1999.

———. *Armageddon: The Cosmic Battle of the Ages.* Wheaton, IL: Tyndale House, 2003.

———. *Assassins: Assignment: Jerusalem, Target: Antichrist.* Wheaton IL: Tyndale House, 1999.

———. *Desecration: Antichrist Takes the Throne.* Wheaton, IL: Tyndale House, 2001.

———. *Glorious Appearing: The End of Days.* Wheaton, IL: Tyndale House, 2004.

———. *Kingdom Come: The Final Victory.* Wheaton, IL: Tyndale House, Inc., 2007.

———. *Left Behind: A Novel of the Earth's Last Days.* Wheaton, IL: Tyndale House, 1995.

———. *Nicolae: The Rise of the Antichrist.* Wheaton, IL: Tyndale House, 1997.

———. *Soul Harvest: The World Takes Sides.* Wheaton, IL: Tyndale House, 1998.

———. *The Indwelling: The Beast Takes Possession.* Wheaton, IL: Tyndale House, 2001.

———. *The Mark: The Beast Who Rules the World.* Wheaton, IL: Tyndale House, 2000.

———. *The Rapture: In the Twinkling of an Eye.* Wheaton, IL: Tyndale House, 2006.

———.*The Regime: Evil Advances Before They Were Left Behind.* Wheaton, IL: Tyndale House, 2005.

———. *The Remnant: On the Brink of Armageddon.* Wheaton, IL: Tyndale House, 2002.

———. *The Rising: Antichrist Is Born Before They Were Left Behind.* Wheaton, IL: Tyndale House, 2005.

———. *Tribulation Force: The Continuing Drama of Those Left Behind.* Wheaton, IL: Tyndale, 1996.

LaHaye, Tim with Steve Halliday. *The Merciful God of Prophecy: His Loving Plans for You in the End Times.* New York: First Warner Books, 2002.

Landis, James. *The Last Day: A Novel.* Hanover, New Hampshire: Steerforth Press, 2009.

Lee, Earl. *Kiss My Left Behind.* Chula Vista, CA: Aventine 2003.

Lindsey, Hal. *Planet Earth—2000 A.D.* Palos Verdes, Calif: Western Front, 1996.

———. *The Late Great Planet Earth.* Grand Rapids, Mich: Zondervan, 1970.

———. *The Rapture: Truth or Consequences.* NY: Bantam, 1983.

Lomborg, Bjorn., editor. *Global Crises, Global Solutions.* Cambridge: Cambridge University Press, 2004.

Long, Thomas G. *Preaching from Memory and Hope.* Louisville: Westminster, 2009.

Love, Julian Price. "Revelation to John," *The Layman's Bible Commentary*, vol. 25. Richmond, VA: John Knox, 1960.

Lumpkin, W. L. *Baptist Confessions of Faith.* Philadelphia: Judson, 1959.

Maahs, Kenneth H. *Of Angels, Beasts and Plagues: The Message of Revelation for a New Millennium.* Valley Forge: Judson, 1999.
MacPherson, Dave. *The Incredible Cover-Up.* Plainfield, NJ: Logos International 1975.
———. *The Rapture Plot.* Simpsonville, SC: Millennium III, 2000.
———.. *The Three R's: Rapture, Revisionism, Robbery: Pretribulation, Rapturism from 1930 to Hal Lindsey.* Simpsonville, SC: P.O.S.T. Inc., 1998.
Malina, Bruce J. and John J. Pilch. *Social-Science Commentary on the Book of Revelation.* Minneapolis: Fortress, 2000.
Marty, Martin E. "Year of the Locust." *The Christian Century,* June 15, 2004, 47.
Maslin, Mark. *Global Warming: A Very Short Introduction.* New York: Oxford University Press, 2004.
McDowell, Edward A. *The Meaning and Message of The Book of Revelation.* Nashville: Broadman, 1951.
McKibben, Bill. "Hot and Bothered: Facing Up to Global Warming," *The Christian Century,* July 11, 2006, 31.
———. *The End of Nature.* New York: Random House, 2006.
Metzger, Bruce. *Breaking the Code.* Nashville: Abingdon, 1993.
Moltmann, Jurgen. *Theology of Hope.* New York: Harper & Row, 1967.
Moody, Dale. *The Word of Truth: A Summary of Christian Doctrine Based on Biblical Revelation.* Grand Rapids: Eerdmans, 1981.
Myers, Allen C. "Antichrist." *The Eerdmans Bible Dictionary.* Grand Rapids, Mich: William B. Eerdmans Publishing Co., 1987.
Oates, Wayne E. "The Daily Providence of God," unpublished sermon, St. Matthews Baptist Church, Louisville, Kentucky, June 24, 1984.
Olson, Carl E. *Will Catholics Be "Left Behind?": A Critique of the Rapture and Today's Prophecy Preachers.* San Francisco: Ignatius, 2003.
———. "Five Myths About the Rapture," *Crisis: Politics, Culture and the Church,* 4–5. www.crisismagazine.com/November2003/Olson.htm.
Otto, Rudolf. *The Idea of the Holy.* New York: Oxford University Press, 1923.
Pannenberg, Wolfhart. *The Apostle's Creed in the Light of Today's Questions.* Philadelphia: Westminster, 1972.
Perkins, Pheme. "The Gospel of Mark," *The New Interpreter's Bible,* vol. VIII. Nashville: Abingdon, 1995.
Phillips, Kevin. *American Theocracy.* New York: Viking, 2006.
Primavesi, Anne. *From Apocalypse to Genesis: Ecology, Feminism and Christianity.* Minneapolis: Fortress, 1991.
Reddish, Mitchell G. *Revelation, Smyth & Helwys Bible Commentary.* Macon, GA: Smyth & Helwys, 2001.
Redditt, Paul L. "Apocalyptic Literature." *Mercer Dictionary of the Bible.* Watson Mills, General Editor. Macon, GA: Mercer University Press, 1990.
Rist, M. "Antichrist," *The Interpreter's Dictionary of the Bible,* A-D. Nashville: Abingdon, 1962.
Robertson, Pat. *Bring It On: Tough Questions, Candid Answers.* Nashville: Word, 2003.
———. *The End of the Age.* Nashville: Word, 2002.
Rogers, Adrian. *Unveiling the End Times in Our Time.* Nashville: Broadman & Holmes, 2004.
Rossing, Barbara R. *The Rapture Exposed: The Message of Hope in the Book of Revelation.* Boulder, CO: Westview, 2004.

———. "God's Unfinished Future: Why It Matters Now," The 37 Annual Trinity Institute, Trinity Church, Wall Street, New York, City, January 23, 2007.
Rowland, Christopher C. "The Book of Revelation," *The New Interpreter's Bible*, vol. XII. Nashville: Abingdon, 1998.
Rust, Eric C. *Nature: Garden or Desert*. Waco, Texas: Word, 1971.
"Samford professor delves into books, film in CFB General Assembly Workshops" / *Wallace@thefellowship.info.*, Tuesday, June 29; 2004.
Schaefer, Francis A. *Pollution and the Death of Man: The Christian View of Ecology*. Wheaton, IL: Tyndale House, 1970.
Scharff, Judith S., editor. *The Mother Earth Handbook*. New York: Continuum, 1991.
Schweizer, Eduard. "Revelation." *A New Handbook of Christian Theology*, edited by Donald W. Musser and Joseph L. Price. Nashville: Abingdon, 1992.
Shepherd, J. Barrie. *A Child Is Born: Mediations for Advent and Christmas*. Philadelphia: Westminster, 1988
Smith, Abraham."The First Letter to the Thessalonians." *The New Interpreter's Bible*, vol. XI. Nashville: Abingdon, 2000.
Strandberg, Todd and Terry James. *Are You Rapture Ready?* New York: A Plume Book, 2004.
"The 25 Most Influential Evangelicals in America," *Time*, February 7, 2005, 39.
*The Virginian-Pilot*. "A Scary Diagnosis for Planet Earth." Tuesday, April 5, 2005.
Tillich, Paul. *Dynamics of Faith*. New York: Harper & Brothers, 1957.
———. *The Protestant Era*. Chicago: Chicago University Press, 1948.
Tuck, William Powell. *Authentic Evangelism: Sharing the Good News with Sense and Sensitivity*. Valley Forge: Judson, 2002.
———. *The Compelling Faces of Jesus*. Macon GA: Mercer University Press, 2008.
Tupper, Frank. *A Scandalous Presence: The Jesus Story of the Compassion of God*. Macon, GA: Mercer University Press, 1995.
Van Impe, Jack. *God's Promises of Prophecy*. Dallas: Word, 1998.
———. *2001: On the Edge of Eternity*. Dallas: Word, 1996.
"Video game for Christians draws criticism," The Associated, *Richmond Times Dispatch*, December 12, 2006.
Vinson, Richard. "The Social World of the Book of Revelation," *Review and Expositor* (98, Winter 2001), 29.
Walker, Williston. *A History of the Christian Church*. New York: Charles Scribner's Sons, 1970.
Walvoord, John F. *End Times*. Nashville: Word, 1998.
———. *The Rapture of the Church*. Grand Rapids: Zondervan, 1957.
———. *The Rapture Question*. Grand Rapids: Zondervan, 1978.
Weart, Spencer R. *The Discovery of Global Warming*. Cambridge, MA: Harvard University Press, 2003.
Wilson, E. O. *The Creation: An Appeal to Save Life on Earth*. New York: W. W. Norton and Company, 2006.
Wilson, Nathan D. *Right Behind: A Parody of Last Days of Goofiness*. Moscow ID: Canon, 2001.
Wink, Walter. *Engaging the Powers: Discernment and Resistance in a World of Domination*. Minneapolis: Fortress, 1992.
Witherington III, Ben. *Revelation*. Cambridge: Cambridge University Press, 2003.

———. "What the Left Behind Series Left Out." *Bible Review*. August 2002, vol. XVIII, no. 4.
Wright, N. T. "Farewell to the Rapture," *Bible Review*, August 2001, vol.XVII no. 4, 8.
———. *Jesus and the Victory of God*. Minneapolis: Fortress, 1996.
———. *Surprised by Hope: Rethinking Heaven, the Resurrection, and the Mission of the Church*. New York: HarperOne, 2008.

# Subject/Name Index

1 Corinthians 71, 76–78, 82, 116, 117, 133, 138
1 Thessalonians 50–51, 71, 73, 75–76, 77, 78, 81ff, 116
144,000 Jewish Witnesses, The 43–44, 57, 104, 114
60 Minutes 7, 10, 19, 49, 109
666 39–40, 56, 59, 61, 119
9/11 xi, 8, 9, 10
Ababneh, Abdullah 121
Abanes, Richard 5
Adhem, Abou Ben xii
Albom, Mitch xiii
Alcott, Louisa May xiii
Allegorical interpretation 59–60, 90
Amillennial 33
Angley, Ernest 8
Antichrist 2, 3, 12, 21, 34–38, 46, 57, 70, 85, 91, 93, 105, 110, 112, 119, 126
Anticipation 142–143
*Apocalypse of Elijah* 14
Apocalypse, The 23, 32, 50, 58, 59, 61, 62, 66, 90, 92, 93, 103, 133
Apocalyptic approach 66–68, 90–96
Apocalyptic Literature 46, 49, 50ff, 86–87, 93, 132
Apostasy 45, 53–54, 62
Aquinas, Thomas 131
Are coming soon 62–63
Armageddon 31, 46, 84, 85, 93, 112
Asbury Theological Seminary 132
Athanasius 131
Augustine 131
Aune, David E. 39
Bakker, Jim 5, 13
Baptist Faith and Message, The 137
Baptist Theological Seminary at Richmond, The xiv

Barclay, William 102, 132
Barnes, Bruce 3, 107, 111
Barr, James 74, 86
Barrigan, Daniel 64
Battle of Armageddon, The 11, 22, 32, 110
Bauckham, Richard 84
Beasley-Murray, George 39, 122
Beast, The 38–40, 59, 60, 61, 91
Ben-Judah, Tsion 4, 110, 112, 113, 119, 126–27
Bernanos, Georges xiii
Bettenson, Henry 137
Billings, Vernon 3, 77, 99, 108, 116, 120
Blake, William 66
Blevins, James L. 65–66, 132
Blomburg, Craig 72
Blount, Brian 64, 103–4
Boesak, Allan 64
Bond, James 124
Boring, Eugene 50, 67, 103, 132
Bowls, The 48
Bowman, John Wick 66
Bradbury, Ray 22
*Breaking the Code* ix
Brokaw, Tom 19
Brown, Dan ix, xiii
Bruce, Kenny 2
Buechner, Frederick xiii
Bullard, Robert 20
Bundick, Sandra xiv
Bush, George W. 1
Buttrick, George xi
Caird, G. B. 104
Calvin, John 131
Campbell, Will xiii
Campolo, Tony 20
Camus, Albert xiii

153

# Subject/Name Index

Carpathia, Nicolae 3, 21, 22, 34, 41, 98, 110, 118–21, 124, 126
Carter, Jimmy 1
Cassandra xi
Cayce, Edward 6
Chesterton, G. K. x
Christ 27, 32, 33, 37, 42, 44, 52, 57, 60, 75, 77–78, 81, 95, 98, 99, 104, 106, 108, 113, 114, 143, 144
*Christian Century, The* 19
Christian growth 130
Christian living 123–24
Christology 37
Church 22, 23, 45, 61, 62, 66–67, 69, 88ff, 95, 104–7, 112–15, 117–18, 138
Clancy, Tom 21
Clemens, Samuel L. xiii
Cobb, John B. Jr. 20
Collins, Adela Yarboro 63–64
Collins, John 91
Commoner, Barry 17
Communion 107–11, 136
Conroy, Pat xiii
Contemporary Historical view 60, 90
Conversion 98, 107–15
Cosmic Dualism 52, 91
Cothran, Todd 22
Couch, Mal 36
Crisis 51–52
*Da Vinci Code, The* ix, xiii
Dallas Theological Seminary 11, 12, 63, 75
Daniel 14, 28, 29, 32, 49, 50, 62, 89–90, 98, 126
Darby, John Nelson 10–14, 29, 63, 71, 72, 74, 86, 88, 89, 129
Day of the Lord 80–81
DeMar, Gary 39, 45, 72, 88, 89, 98
Dennis Miller Show, The 7
Denver Conservative Baptist Seminary 72
Dinallo, Grey 6
Dispensation 10, 11, 24–25, 27, 29, 73, 75–76, 89, 105, 116, 126, 129
Dixon, Jeane 6
Doctrines, Christian 69, 136–37
Dodge, Mary Mapes xiii

Domitian 39, 51, 54
Doomsday 5
Doomsday Preachers 10–16, 49
Dramatic literary view 64–66, 90
Dualism 35–36, 52–53, 123
Durer, Albrecht 66
Durham, Hattie 4, 21, 108, 111
Dyer, Charles H. 5
Eastern Baptist Theological Seminary 72
Ecology 17–21
Edwards, Denis 20
Ehrlich, Paul 20
Eiseley, Loren 134
Elder, Frederick 20
Ellul, Jacque 103
End Times, The 8, 25, 28, 31–32, 49, 59, 90
Enigma Babylon One World Faith 3, 124–25
Eschatology 11, 31, 58ff, 68, 129
Evangelism 109–16
Evans, Michael D. 5
Evil 37, 52–53, 57, 85, 140–41
Ezekiel 2, 22, 50, 56
False Prophet, The 3, 41
Falwell, Jerry 2, 8, 13, 63, 74, 105
Faulkner, William xiii
Fidelity 53–54, 60, 67, 87, 100, 129–30, 139–44
First Confession, The 137
Florenza, Elisabeth Schussler 64
Forgiveness 122
Fortunato, Leon 3, 41
Fosdick, Harry Emerson xi
Four Horsemen, The 47, 111
Four Living Creatures 56
Frykholm, Amy Johnson 114–15
Fundamentalism 5, 74
Futurist view of end times 62–63, 90, 92, 93
Girzone, Joseph F. xiii
Global warming 18–21
Glorious Appearing, The 10, 24, 27, 33, 42, 116, 120, 126
Gnostic 16

## Subject/Name Index 155

God 10, 42, 52, 53, 54–55, 57, 78, 87, 98–100, 107, 119–22, 127, 131, 133ff, 142, 144
Golden, William 69
Gore, Al 18–19
Gossip, A. J. xi
Graham, Billy 92
Great Apostasy, The 44–45
Great Tribulation, The 41–42, 77
Greene, Graham xiii
Grey, Zane xiii
Grisham, John xiii, 8
Hagee, John 5
Hall, Douglas John 131
Hall, James xiii
Hammarskjold, Dag 135
Hampshire Confession, The 137
Hansen, James 19
Hargrove, Eugene C. 20
Heaven 10, 31, 73, 75, 91, 93
Hegel 130–31
Hell 91, 131
Helms, Hal M. 144
Hemmingway, Ernest xiii
Hendriksen, William 88
Historical approach 61–62
Historical time out 89–90
Hitchcock, Albert 22
Hitchcock, Mark 5
Houghton, John 18
Hull, William E. 73, 78
Hunt, Leigh xii
Hunter, George G. 111, 115
Hyatt, Michael S. 15
Ice, Thomas 5
II Enoch 14
Isaiah 14, 32, 87, 101
James, Terry 109
Jeremiah, David 5
Jerusalem 42
Jewish Temple, The 36, 41–42
Jews 50–51, 114, 126–27
Joel 32, 50
John, Gospel of 6, 71, 78–79, 100, 101, 116, 117, 137
Johannine Epistles, The 36–37, 99, 100
Joyner, Rick 5

Judgment 47, 48, 91, 93, 118–22, 126
Kafka, Franz xiii
Keener, Craig S. 72
Killinger, John xii, xiii
King, Larry 19, 32
King, Stephen 8
Kirban, Salem 8
Koontz, Dean xiii
Koresh, David 9
Lamb, The 55, 100–4, 105, 106, 121
Landis, James 5
Last days 6, 46
Last things 31–32, 49, 58
Lee, Earl 128
Lewis, C. S. xiii
Liberty University 74, 75
Lindsey, Hal x, 9, 12, 71, 73–74, 105, 109, 112, 129
Literal interpretation of Scripture 30–31, 83–86, 93, 94
Little Apocalypse of Mark 36
Lomborg, Bjorn 20
Long, Thomas 68
Love, Julian Price 91, 132
Luke, Gospel of 6, 51
Lumpkin, William 137
Luther, Martin 61, 131
Maahs, Kenneth H. 39, 60, 91, 95–96, 132
MacDonald, Margaret 10
MacPherson, Dave 10
Mark of the Beast, The 40–41, 43, 48, 108–9, 118–22
Mark, Gospel of 6, 51, 141
Martin, Claude 17
Matthew, Gospel of 30, 51, 78, 79–80, 106, 116
Matthews, Peter 3
McDowell, Edward A. 65
McKibben, Bill 19
Megiddo 46
Metzger, Bruce ix
Michener, James xiii
Millennial Madness 14–16
Millennium bug 14
Millennium, The 6, 27, 33–34, 121
Moltmann, Jürgen 116–17

## Subject/Name Index

Moody, Dale 139
Moral Majority 74
*Mysterium Tremendum* 136
Mystery 133–36
Nag Hammadi ix
National Council of Churches, The 44, 125–27
Nature out of Control 16–21
Nero 39, 51
New Babylon 35, 42–43, 48, 126
New Hope Village Church 3, 77, 107, 111, 113
New Testament, The 26, 117–18
*New York Times* 6, 15
*Newsweek* 7, 14
Nicene Creed, The 137
Nordhoff, Charles xiii
Nostradamus 6
Numinous Other 136
Oates, Wayne 139
Oilar, Forrest Loman 7
Olson, Carl E. 72–73, 126, 139
Oppenheimer, Michael 19
Origen 59
Panmillennialists 33–34
Pannenburg, Wolfhart 116
*Parousia* 80–84
Past Tense view 60–62, 90
Pasternak, Boris xiii
Paton, Alan xiii
Paul 37, 76, 81–83, 102, 116, 131, 138, 139, 140
*Pax Christi* 106
*Pax Romana* 106
Persecution 51–52, 62, 91, 92, 139–40
Pessimism 53
Philadelphia Confession, The 137
Phillips, Bob 7
Phillips, Kevin 1
Political religious typology 63–64
Pontifex Maximus 3, 45, 124
Postmillennialist 33, 72, 74
Potter, Harry ix
Predicting the remote future 61–62
Premillennialist 24–25, 33, 34, 74
*Preterite* 60, 66

Pretribulation 10, 28, 33, 72, 73, 74–75, 80, 88, 96–98
Prophecy 61, 94–95
Protestant Principle, The 131
Providence of God 54–55, 100
Pseudonymous authorship 55–56
Publishers Weekly 6
Pyles, Howard xiii
Rapture, The 8, 10, 25–27, 32, 70ff, 81, 83, 109, 111, 113, 116–18, 129, 137
Reddish, Mitchell 39, 46, 50, 73, 91, 103, 132
Remote Future prediction 61, 90
Resources 132–33
Resurrection 75, 77, 79, 116–18, 137–39
Revelation, Book of 2, 5, 13, 28, 29, 31, 32, 33, 49, 51, 57–58, 67, 87–96, 97, 100, 122, 129
Ridicule 127–28
Robertson, Pat 5, 9, 13, 105, 109
Rogers, Adrian 109
Roman Catholics 26, 61, 87, 125–26
Rose, Lee 113
Rosenzweig, Chaim 3, 4, 84, 98, 107, 111, 126
Rossing, Barbara R. 74, 76, 122, 124
Rowland, Christopher C. 85, 122, 132
Rowling, J. K. ix, x, 22
Ruby, Lisa 127–28
Rust, Eric 20
Salvation 98, 107–9
Samford University 73
Satan xi, 12, 52, 57, 105
Schaefer, Francis A. 20
Schweitzer, Albert 131
Schweizer, Eduard 139
*Scofield Reference Bible* 12
Scofield, C. I. x, 63, 86, 88
Second Coming, The 26–27, 28, 29, 42, 45, 60, 71, 73, 80–81, 116, 139
Seven Churches, The 88–89
Seven Year Tribulation, The 29–30, 62–63, 90
Shaw, George Bernard 143
Shepherd, Barrie 121
Single Parousia 80–83

Socio-political 95–96
Southeastern Baptist Theological
  Seminary 65
Southern Baptist Theological Seminary,
  The 65, 73
Spong, John Shelby 44–45
St. Matthews Baptist Church 102, 139
Stanton, Gerald B. 11
Steel, Danielle 8
Steele, Chloe 2, 21, 70, 99, 107–8, 110,
  111, 112, 120, 123
Steele, Irene 2
Steele, Rayford 2, 21, 70, 85, 99, 107–8,
  111, 112, 113, 114, 120, 123
Steele, Raymie 2, 112
Steinbeck, John xiii
Stevenson, Robert Louis xiii
Stonagal, Jonathan 22
Strandberg, Todd 109
Street, James xiii
Suffering Servant 27, 101, 103
Swanson, Sandi L. 4
Sword, The 84ff, 103
Symbolism 56, 58, 59, 66, 85, 92, 93, 94,
  96, 102
Terrorist Threat 8–10
*The Late Great Planet Earth* 12
*The Spire* 69–70
Thieme, Robert 12
Tiberias, Naomi 3, 23
Tillich, Paul 131
*Time Magazine* 1, 14, 16
Time/CNN 8
Titus 116
Tolkien, J. R. R. xiii
Transaction 108
Tribulation Force 2, 3, 21, 22, 31, 97, 104,
  106, 111–12, 113, 120, 123
Trinity Institute 122
Trumpets, The 47
Tuck, William xi, 115
Tupper, Frank 143
Turner, J. M. W. 66
Twain, Mark xiii
Two Ages 52
Two Witnesses 43
Unger, Merrill F. 12

Union Theological Seminary 125
Updike, John xiii
*USA Today* 6
Van Impe, Jack 5, 13, 16, 105
Vinson, Richard B. xiv, 51–52, 83
Visions 56
*Wall Street Journal, The* 6
Wallace, Lew xiii
Wells, H. G. xiii
Wesley, John 131
Westminster Confession of Faith, The
  137
White Horse 84–86
Whitty, Catherine xiv
Williams, Cameron (Buck) 2, 3, 43, 70,
  98, 108, 111, 120, 123, 124
Willow Creek Community Church 115
Wilson, Nathan D. 128
Witherington, Ben III 71–71, 73, 92,
  122, 132
Wolvoord, John F. 11, 63
Wong, Chang 3, 21
World Council of Churches, The 44, 92,
  125–27
Wright, N. T. 76. 80
Y2K Problem 14–16
Zechariah 32, 50

www.ingramcontent.com/pod-product-compliance
Lightning Source LLC
Chambersburg PA
CBHW072138160426
43197CB00012B/2158